Vancouver

Berlitz
Vancouver

Original text by Paula Tevis
Edited by Media Content Marketing, Inc.
Photography by Doug Plummer
Cover photograph by Stuart Dee
Layout by Media Content Marketing, Inc.
Cartography by Ortelius Design
Managing Editor: Tony Halliday

Second Edition 2002 (Reprinted 2004)

CONTACTING THE EDITORS
Every effort has been made to provide accurate information in this publication, but changes are inevitable. The publisher cannot be responsible for any resulting loss, inconvenience or injury. We would appreciate it if readers would call our attention to any errors or outdated information by contacting Berlitz Publishing, PO Box 7910, London SE1 1WE, England. Fax: (44) 20 7403 0290;
e-mail: berlitz@apaguide.co.uk; www.berlitzpublishing.com

100/302 RP

CONTENTS

● All prices are in Canadian dollars

● A 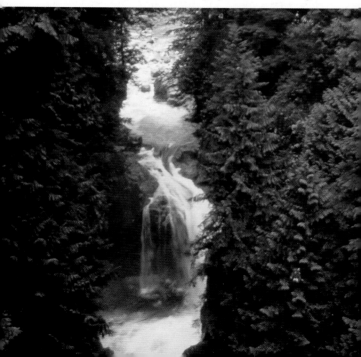 in the text denotes a highly recommended sight

Vancouver

VANCOUVER AND ITS PEOPLE

Imagine for a moment that you are on a broad walkway that winds along a boat-filled harbor. As you relax on a smooth wood bench, your eyes rest on a great swath of forest a stone's throw away. An endless stretch of mountains, woolly with trees, provides the background a few miles north, beckoning past the dark blue waters of the inlet that divides the shores. Behind you, the late afternoon sun has transformed a dozen glass high-rises into glistening emerald-, ruby-, and sapphire-toned baubles. Now turn east along the bay, catching sight of five enormous white sails that majestically anchor the tip of downtown, and the next thing you know, you are completely infatuated with Vancouver.

Canada's third-largest city is a visual delight no matter where you linger, but it's more than just a pretty face. Vancouver works hard to maximize the beauty of its surroundings. Multi-story office, condominium, and apartment buildings dominate the skyline, yet their occupants nearly always enjoy a view of the mountains or sea from a multitude of windows and the requisite balcony. On busy downtown streets, merely walk a block or so—or simply turn your head—and you'll be treated to the sight of the Coast mountains, the splendors of Stanley Park, the waters of Burrard Inlet, or all three if you're particularly well situated. Notice, too, what isn't there. Trash, for instance. Here you have an urban, densely populated, popular destination and it's clean. Even the air smells delicious. And note the lack of freeways zigzagging about. While there is no shortage of automobiles, the powers-that-be bowed to the demands of an occasionally vocal majority and eschewed mazes of concrete

Music in the air — on the litter-free sidewalks of Vancouver, even the street musicians are clean.

for clear vistas. An efficient choice? Perhaps not. A thoughtful and appropriate one? Oh, yes.

Rather than encourage even more automobiles by building those freeways, city planners for the Greater Vancouver Regional District implemented ideas for mixed-use zoning and modest transit options that would lead to several sophisticated commercial areas rather than only one. Vancouver itself deliberately rezoned downtown land for residential use, resulting over the years in the development of vibrant neighborhoods as exemplified by the West End, Yaletown, and False Creek. The result is a compact, easy-to-absorb, simple-to-navigate, open, and accessible city that is conscious of its charms and careful to preserve them.

Mistakes were made, naturally, such as the demolition in the 1960s of older single-family homes in the West End to make way for unattractive litters of apartment towers, but for the most part the city recognizes its treasures. This can sometimes be credited to foresight. Stanley Park surely started the blood rushing through many an ambitious developer in the early days, yet the original city council's first vote was to lease these 405 hectares (1,000 acres) from the federal government for a park. Sometimes it can be traced to imagination. Granville Island was little more than an industrial wasteland after World War II, until a group of politicians and business-people in the early 1970s envisioned it for public use and created one of the most popular destinations in the entire city for both locals and tourists.

In other cases, these decisions are due to a confluence of luck and timing. Pacific Spirit Park, part of the university's endowment lands, was saved from becoming a housing tract through a combination of unfortunate circumstances (unfortunate for the would-be developers, that is) and community activism. Vancouverites may claim to be politically apathetic, but they know when to rally around a good cause.

The city's half-million residents (with another 1.9 million in the Greater Vancouver metropolitan area) represent an amalgam of cultures from Europe, Asia, Latin America, and British Columbia's indigenous population. Fully 50 percent of Greater Vancouver residents are Asian. After English, Mandarin Chinese is the language most often spoken. The treatment by the early ruling class of many ethnic groups (particularly the Chinese prior to 1947, the Japanese at the turn of the century and during World War II, and the Sikhs in 1914) left much to be desired, but over the years Vancouver has evolved. The city is considered not only a bastion for tolerance and acceptance, but a model. And despite the multiculturalism, or more likely because of it, some delightful, all-pervasive local ethic provides the tie that binds. (Maybe it's something in the water?) Vancouverites, no matter where they hail from, bear a well-deserved reputation for being amazingly friendly, polite, and open-minded. They are also rather modest, often crediting their fine traits as being somehow "Canadian" in nature.

A second principle the locals live by has to do with being outdoors as often as possible. Vancouverites work hard, but they play much harder, tackling their days off with all the exuberance of grade-schoolers let out for recess. Walking, running, hiking, in-line skating, swimming, kayaking, sailing, skiing—when a sports-obsessed citizen flips open the ubiquitous cellular phone, chances are he or she is setting up a jogging date rather than a meeting. And the weather is no excuse to cancel. The folks here don't change their plans because of rain, even with an average of 170 days of drizzle annually. A reputation for wet weather notwithstanding, Vancouver boasts the mildest climate of any Canadian city. This is one reason why so many residents have moved here from other parts of the nation.

Along with its good-natured citizenry and glorious location, the city's appeal also lies in the fact that it retains a small-town sensibility despite its status as a major port and trading partner in the Pacific Rim. The engaging neighborhoods, from trendy Yaletown to the more traditional Point Grey, each can be accurately characterized in a sentence, and you can visit them all in a day, practically on foot. Drivers stop (not just slow down) for pedestrians, and they take turns merging on the Lions Gate Bridge during rush hour. Since you can't really tell the tourists from the locals, drop by the same coffee bar two mornings in a row and you'll be considered a regular.

In reality though, Vancouver is a big city, and like all big cities it has an underbelly. Vancouver's importance as a world port is both a blessing and a bit of a curse. Alaskan cruise ships make regular use of Vancouver's berths, annually contributing over $300 million to the economy and depositing over 800,000 passengers downtown for a day or more of shopping and sightseeing. Container shipping is big business as well, and billions of dollars worth of goods pass

Cycling is a popular pursuit among environmentally conscious and athletically active Vancouverites.

through Vancouver on their way to Japan, China, and other Pacific Rim destinations.

At the same time, busy ports attract the drug trade. Vancouver has always been a hot spot for trafficking, and opium users were a source of civic shame back at the turn of the 20th century. Decades later they've been replaced by cocaine and heroin addicts, whom the city attempts to control by corralling them inside the downtown East Side. Canada's sane gun-control laws help keep major crime in check, however. Vehicle break-ins are actually the most common aggravation anyone faces in Vancouver, one that is easily solved by keeping the car's interior devoid of anything worth pawning.

Engaging in controversy over the drug issue (or anything else, for that matter) isn't considered a popular sport among the general public. Frosting the city's overall character, like winter snow on Grouse Mountain, is the terminally laid-back atmosphere. If New York City is suits and attitude, and Los Angeles is sunglasses and tummy tucks, Vancouver is, well, cargo pants and polar fleece. Or shorts and sandals, depending on the thermometer. No one is too hurried to give directions, admonitions to walk your bike on certain parts of the seawall path are given gently, and there's no attitude delivered with the restaurant specials. As one booster put it, "We're just into living."

They must be onto something. In 1997, the Corporate Resources Group of Geneva, Switzerland, ranked Vancouver as the best city in the world in which to live, and in that same year *Condé Nast Traveler* readers voted Vancouver one of the top ten destinations to visit. In 1998, *Travel and Leisure* included Vancouver in its top-ten list. Along with the accolades come more and more tourists—7.8 million per year at last count—and Vancouver continues to work on the infrastructure to accommodate the visiting throngs. The next few years will bring more hotels, a new conference center, and another cruise ship terminal. It will likely bring additional restaurants to the flourishing food panoply, although with more than 3,000 eateries to choose from, that might be gilding the grilled salmon.

Little of this crosses one's mind, however, when sitting on a neatly placed log on the sand overlooking English Bay, with the sun drifting into the sea. The overwhelming beauty that has caught your eye, your imagination, and your heart in the first place is all absorbing and, indeed, all you really need to know about Vancouver.

The five white sails of Canada Place are among the many glorious landmarks that might help to orient you in the city.

A BRIEF HISTORY

In the Beginning

Archaeological evidence indicates that First Nations peoples have lived in British Columbia (BC) for as long as 10,000 years and in Vancouver for at least 3,000. Prior to contact with Europeans in the 1700s, these Coast Salish tribes lived in seasonal encampments on Burrard Inlet and English Bay, on the shores of North Vancouver, and on the Fraser River, whose arms surround the city of Richmond. Within present-day Vancouver itself, Squamish and Musqueam Natives maintain settlements in the areas around Jericho Beach in the Point Grey neighborhood, at Kitsilano Point near today's Vanier Park, and in Stanley Park where Lumberman's Arch now stands.

A dependable supply of salmon, shellfish, and plant life provided the Indians with plenty of food. In turn, this bounty allowed them the leisure to hone sophisticated skills such as wood carving and to develop ceremonial customs to celebrate marriages, births, and alliances. One such practice was the potlatch, in which entire tribes would be entertained lavishly at huge gatherings planned years in advance. Such a ceremony aided in transmitting news and stories to attendees and conferred great status on the hosts.

It is not known precisely how many Coast Salish Natives lived in Vancouver, but smallpox epidemics are blamed for decimating a majority of the population in the 1700s and early 1800s. Those who survived encountered a small but steady stream of explorers to the territory, beginning with the Spaniard José Maria Narvarez in 1791. He was quickly followed by Captain George Vancouver in 1792. Representing Great Britain, Vancouver arrived with the two-fold intention of mapping the Northwest Coast and negotiating with Narvaez's successor, Juan Francisco de la Bodega y Quadra, regarding a dispute involving Spain's capture of three British ships in 1789. Vancouver spent three consecutive summers surveying the coast, naming over 400 places including Vancouver Island. (He originally called it "Quadra and Vancouver Island" to commemorate his friendly relationship with the rival captain.) It would be another 90 years before the mainland would bear his name as well.

From Fur to Fish to Forests

Fur trading brought the first group of English settlers to the Greater Vancouver area in 1827. These employees of the Hudson's Bay Company built Fort Langley on the Fraser River, approximately 50 km (31 miles) from today's Vancouver. The lucrative fur trade was equaled and soon surpassed by salmon exports in the 1840s, when Fort Langley was the largest exporter of fish on the Pacific Coast. Despite these early business successes, it was the 1858 announcement that gold had been discovered in the Fraser River that spurred the British, who

Totem poles in Stanley Park conjure up the 8,000-year presence of First Nations people in the BC vicinity.

already were governing Vancouver Island (calling it "British Columbia"), to declare the mainland a colony as well. They did so in response to the 25,000-plus gold diggers from the United States who converged on the river, still seeking the riches that had eluded them back in California during the Gold Rush of 1849.

Despite the hordes of prospectors making their way through the largely unsettled mainland, the European population around Burrard Inlet still consisted of a single hardy soul. To encourage growth, the governor of Vancouver Island, James Douglas, initiated a law allowing Europeans to appropriate land not settled by Native peoples, who, as fate would have it, had defined but small, summer and winter settlements. This offer encouraged three English prospectors to clear a plot of land near what is now the West End of the city. Vancouver was finally off to a start, if not a particularly rousing one.

The Roedde House Museum in Barclay Square Heritage Park traces Vancouver's past.

In 1867, the first mill on the south shore opened just blocks from the heart of today's Gastown at the end of Dunlevy Street. Originally named for its owner, Edward Stamp, it later became Hastings Mill; the village around it took the name Hastings Township. That same year, Canada officially became a country and John Deighton paddled into Burrard Inlet with a small entourage and a keg of whiskey. At the time, the closest bar was an inconvenient half day's walk away. "Gassy Jack," as the garrulous Deighton became known, was persuasive enough—or the mill workers were thirsty enough—to convince the settlers to build him a saloon within 24 hours of his arrival, and Gastown, as the settlement was soon nicknamed, was on the map.

The Railroad Arrives

While the land closer to the Fraser River was peopled with farmers and fishermen, there wasn't much to Gastown (officially known as "Granville"), outside of Gassy Jack's hotel-saloon, 22 other saloons, the brothels, the mill, and a few stores and houses. This was all poised to change in 1871, when the province of British Columbia linked its fate with Canada and joined the Confederation. BC's provincial government did so on a promise from the powerful Canadian Pacific Railway (CPR) to extend its reach into the hinterlands. A second promise by the government to gift the CPR 2,428

John "Gassy Jack" Deighton, the city's original saloon keeper, stands immortalized in Gastown.

hectares (6,000 acres) on Burrard Peninsula sealed the deal to make Granville the railway's terminus.

The CPR's then-general manager, William Van Horne, is credited with renaming scruffy Granville "Vancouver," in his opinion a much grander name that was more befitting the town's future. Vancouver incorporated in 1886, city councilors were elected, and their initial piece of business resulted in the acquisition of a lease for a military reserve that they wanted to develop as a park—Stanley Park, in fact. Two months later, a rogue fire destroyed the ragtag settlement, and Vancouver, with its new name, its new city government, and its new status as the end of the rail line, started its new life by rebuilding from scratch.

Vancouver in the 20th Century

The somewhat sedate and well-ordered Vancouver of the new millennium is quite a contrast to the rough-and-tumble town that quickly sprouted from the ashes of the great fire. From the beginning, Vancouver's explosive growth was accompanied by less-than-exemplary behavior from a good many citizens. Prostitution, which had gained an early foothold in the economy, found bedfellows in gambling and opium dens, and Vancouverites were reported to imbibe more alcohol per capita than any other Canadians. But a semblance of sophistication also found its way into town: Sarah Bernhardt performed at the Vancouver Opera House in 1891; the Carnegie Library at Hastings and Main streets was erected in 1903 (it's now a community center); and the first skyscraper, the Dominion Trust Building on Hastings and Cambie streets, went up in 1909. By 1911, the suburbs surrounding Vancouver, including Richmond, South Vancouver, and Point Grey, were connected to town by electric streetcars that brought 100,000 passengers daily to work and shop.

Chinatown

Of all the immigrants flooding into Vancouver, the Chinese had a particularly difficult time as the targets of severe racial enmity, not unlike their experiences in 19th- and early 20th-century California. As early as 1858, many Chinese migrated from San Francisco to Vancouver seeking gold, and their numbers increased dramatically—to 17,000 between 1881 and 1885—drawn by jobs laying railway tracks. Settling around Carrall and Pender streets (today's Chinatown), they suffered humiliation for decades. The Chinese were victims of discriminatory laws that prevented them from working on government-financed projects, levied a head tax, and eventually prohibited immigration altogether except in very specific cases. In 1907, anti-Chinese riots caused massive destruction in Chinatown.

Yet the Chinese community persevered. They formed "benevolent societies" to assist one another and fight the laws that unfairly restricted their numbers. Finally, the 1923 Chinese Immigration Act was repealed in 1947 and Chinese once again moved to Vancouver, eventually making its Chinatown the largest in Canada and the third largest in North America. A more recent wave of immigration took place when wealthy Hong Kong Chinese relocated to Vancouver prior to the repossession of Hong Kong by China in 1997. After building elaborate homes and investing money in real estate and other investments, a fair number have since returned to their homeland after realizing that it's more profitable, and easier, to conduct business in Hong Kong.

Asians now make up 50 percent of the population in the Greater Vancouver area. Their numbers and influence, combined with the city's prominence as a Pacific Rim port, have produced a new generation of business and civic leaders.

19

With World War I came a reduction in trade and the end of the mining boom in the province, but the following decade brought new growth. The largest dance-hall in BC was built on Bowen Island in 1921, and the University of British Columbia finally moved to its new Point Grey campus in 1925, ten years after classes had first begun. Point Grey and South Vancouver merged with Vancouver in 1928, adding another 80,000 people to the roster and making Vancouver the third-largest city in Canada.

During the Great Depression of the 1930s, destitute people from all over the provinces migrated to Vancouver hoping to find work, although there was little to be had. Despite the crash, progress crept along. A new city hall was built out in the "sticks" at 12th and Cambie streets, the Vancouver Art Gallery opened, and the Lions Gate Bridge united West Vancouver and Stanley Park in 1938.

World War II curtailed unemployment in Canada as it did in all of North America, but the bombing of Pearl Harbor led to the internment of Japanese-Canadians. In particular, this changed the demographics of Steveston, a village along the Fraser River where many Japanese fishermen and cannery workers lived and worked. A more hopeful note was sounded in 1947, when Chinese and East Indians were given the vote in provincial elections, followed in 1949 by the enfranchisement of Japanese and the Native populations.

As Vancouver settled into the calm of the post-war 1950s, the population began shifting from the city to the suburbs, with less than half of the 800,000-plus residents of the Greater Vancouver metropolitan area actually residing inside the city's limits. In recognition of the North Shore's growing

Though it appears much older, Gastown's original Steam Clock dates back to its construction in 1977.

influence, the first Canadian shopping mall was built, in well-to-do West Vancouver, and the Lions Gate Bridge changed from private to public ownership.

Hippies discovered the West Side neighborhood of Kitsilano in the 1960s, and developers changed the face of the West End from a neighborhood of single family homes to a high-density enclave of apartment towers and condominiums. Local protests over a proposed downtown freeway muzzled a plan to cut through the East Side's Strathcona neighborhood in this decade as well. Activism at the grassroots level progressed on other issues and precipitated the birth of the environmental group Greenpeace and the rebirth of the long-neglected Gastown district, the city's birthplace.

The One Million Mark

The 1971 census proclaimed a million residents in the Greater Vancouver region. Some of the city's most interesting and popular sites were built during this decade, such as the Museum of Anthropology, Granville Island, the Van Dusen Botanical Gardens, the Stanley Park seawall, and the Steam Clock in Gastown. Vancouver also launched the world's first festival specifically for children in 1978, one of many celebrations that continue to add vibrancy and excitement to the city.

But it took one event in particular, Expo '86, to catapult Vancouver into the international spotlight. To mark the city's 100th birthday, over 22 million visitors from 44 countries dropped by for the 165-day celebration honoring a "World in Motion, World in Touch." Canada Place and its trademark five white sails, Science World (also known as "the golf ball"), and SkyTrain, the city's light-rail rapid transit system, were among the party favors dispensed by Expo. But its most enduring legacy was raising Vancouver's handsome profile. The town hasn't been the same since.

Over 107,000 people have moved into the city during the 1980s and 1990s, reversing a decades-long flow to the suburbs. To accommodate and even encourage this trend, new neighborhoods are in the planning and construction stage. The nearby ski resort of Whistler is even in the running for the 2010 Winter Olympic Games. Trade with Asia, despite the recession, continues to grow, complemented by new markets in South America. And all over the extended city of just under 2 million residents, sustainable growth and opportunity continue to be the watchwords. After 120 years nothing, and everything, has changed.

In Vanier Park the Hastings Mill Store, dating back to 1865, still stands as a catch-all museum of historical relics.

Historical Landmarks

1792   Captain George Vancouver explores Burrard Inlet.

1858   Gold seekers head for the Fraser River.

1867   Stamp's Mill opens at the end of what is now Dunlevy Street in Vancouver. "Gassy Jack" Deighton opens a saloon nearby.

1870   Granville, aka "Gastown," is officially recognized by the provincial government.

1871   British Columbia joins the Federation of Canada.

1872   First school opens on the grounds of Hastings, formerly Stamp's Mill.

1876   A road is built between Granville and Hastings Mill.

1884   William Van Horne, general manager of the CPR, recommends Granville as the terminus of the railroad's western line and recommends renaming the town "Vancouver."

1885   Anti-Chinese immigration act receives royal assent.

1886   Granville incorporates as the City of Vancouver. Fire destroys the town. Three months later, Vancouver's first bank opens.

1887   Whites attack Chinese camp in False Creek. The first Hotel Vancouver opens.

1888   Stanley Park officially opens.

1898   Vancouver population reaches 25,000.

1907   The Vancouver Stock Exchange is incorporated.

1909   First skyscraper is completed at Hastings and Cambie (Dominion Trust Building). Ferry service to West Vancouver begins.

1914	Sikhs refused entry into Vancouver after waiting on board ship for over three months.
1917	Steveston canneries go into decline as a result of the 1913 rock slides that ruined the Fraser River sockeye salmon run.
1926	The Grouse Mountain Chalet opens.
1932	Large numbers of unemployed citizens demonstrate at City Hall.
1938	Lions Gate Bridge opens between Vancouver and West Vancouver.
1942	After bombing of Pearl Harbor, Japanese detainees sent to BC interior.
1948	First television broadcast received.
1959	Oakridge Shopping Centre, Queen Elizabeth Theatre, and Vancouver Maritime Museum open for business.
1971	Gastown is designated an historic site.
1986	Expo '86, the largest special-category world exposition ever staged in North America, takes place in Vancouver, giving rise to Canada Place. Held on the north shore of False Creek, it attracts 22 million visitors.
1993	Boris Yeltsin and Bill Clinton hold an introductory summit in Vancouver to discuss emergency aid for Russia.
1997	Vancouver hosts the Asia–Pacific Economic Cooperation (APEC) summit.

WHERE TO GO

Vancouver is composed of neighborhoods with personalities so distinct that you really don't need a map to tell you when you've crossed the boundaries from one to another. It might be the slight shift in style that tips you off when, for example, South Granville's antiques stores give way to Kitsilano's kitchenware emporiums, or it might be a more obvious shift in cultures as you make your way through the narrow aisles of Chinatown groceries toward the alfresco tables of Commercial Drive coffee houses.

The juxtaposition of varied styles and cultures would be enough to make Vancouver an entertaining destination, but of course the city has the added bonus of an exquisite natural setting. The land and the sea contribute so much of what makes the city immensely desirable that, even when you are confined inside four walls, the local architects have done their best to make everyone acutely conscious of what lies beyond the windows or above the skylights.

Wherever you choose to go in Vancouver, it is likely the outdoors will be an integral part of your plans. Ideally, you'll want to approach your destination wearing a comfortable pair of shoes, for, like all great cities, Vancouver is designed for exploration on foot. Urban planners have provided pedestrians with delightful roads to tread. A truly determined walker (or cyclist) could start on an approximately 22-km (13½-mile) path at Canada Place that eventually leads around Stanley Park and English Bay, circles False Creek, and finishes at Kitsilano Beach for a well-deserved soak in the bay. A more idyllic—and certainly less strenuous—day could begin with a stroll in one of Vancouver's downtown neighborhoods such as Yaletown or the West End, leaving plenty of time for coffee, people-watching, gazing off into

From Stanley Park, you can enjoy views of the Vancouver skyline reaching upward across the water.

the distance, and a lunch break, followed by an afternoon featuring more of the same. Ultimately, it doesn't matter whether you choose style or substance, for there's no such thing as a wasted day in Vancouver.

STANLEY PARK AND THE WEST END

Even the briefest visit to Vancouver has to include a trip to Stanley Park. Located next to the vibrant West End between English Bay and Burrard Inlet, it's one of the loveliest, most entertaining, and memorable spots around.

Stanley Park

A walk or drive through **Stanley Park** shows why this verdant oasis is regarded as the soul of the city. You can begin by the seawall, but really any spot will do. If you can borrow or rent bicycles (rental shops abound on Denman Street), you can tour all of the park's highlights in less than a day.

Named after then-Governor General Lord Stanley, Stanley Park became Vancouver's favorite 405 hectares (1,000 acres) on 17 September 1888, a mere two years after the city officially came into existence. Once thick with cypress, cedar, and Douglas fir trees, its forest and shores were the Native Coast Salish people's hunting and gathering grounds for centuries before smallpox decimated the indigenous population. European settlers then put restrictions on where the remaining Salish could live. In 1863 the area became a military reserve, and five years later logging companies began harvesting the old-growth forest. In 1886, Vancouver's first city council petitioned the federal government to lease the now-unused military reserve to the city for a park. Among the stories about the negotiations that established the park is that the plan gained momentum when an influential land speculator realized that leaving such spectacular acreage unspoiled would only add to the value of his adjacent land. Whether it evolved from self-interest or enlightenment, from its very beginnings the park has shown how quality-of-life and business interests can work in harmony to benefit everyone—a model that has influenced the city's development to this day.

> **Vancouverites are friendly, but they won't initiate a conversation. If you need advice or directions, ask.**

Devonian Harbour Park is the small, flower-bedecked area above Coal Harbour, which leads to the formal entrance to Stanley Park at the foot of West Georgia Street. You'll see a bronze statue of a woman rummaging through her pocketbook (*The Search*, by J. Seward Johnson, Jr.), one of many examples of public art throughout the city. Any runners you see are headed to the seawall promenade, a 10-km (6-mile) path that rings the park and is an all-seasons attraction for strollers, dog walkers, joggers, skaters, and bikers. Along the east side of the promenade are various well-known landmarks including the Vancouver Rowing Club, Royal Vancouver Yacht Club, and the "9 o'clock Gun," which once served as a signal for fishermen and continues to remind the citizenry to put the kids to bed. Before venturing on past Brockton Point and the *Girl in Wetsuit* sculpture, veer off the path to see a collection of Kwakiutl, Tlingit, and Haida totem poles, among the most photographed sites in the city.

Kids of all kinds enjoy the rustic surroundings of the Children's Farmyard in Stanley Park.

Vancouver Highlights (see also pages 42-43)

If you have only a day or two to explore the city, here's a list of the "must-sees" and "must-dos" to help organize your time.

Places to See

Museum of Anthropology: Contains one of the finest collections of First Nations artifacts, displayed in a soaring building on the University of British Columbia campus (see page 51).

Stanley Park: The city's playground and most recognized landmark. Walk the seawall promenade; find Lost Lagoon; mingle with the locals (see page 27).

Granville Island: A reclaimed industrial area turned into a public market, artists' colony, and entertainment complex. Great views. Arrive by ferry and avoid the parking problems (see page 44).

Yaletown: An example of modern Vancouver's neighborhood planning, this four-block area is lively and livable, with great restaurants and shopping (see page 45).

Dr. Sun-Yat-Sen Classical Chinese Garden: The first authentic Suzhou-style garden ever built outside China. Guided tours bring it to life. Try driving or taking a cab there by way of **Gastown**, just to be able to say you saw that historical but, frankly, touristy section of downtown (see page 40).

Places to Stroll

Canada Place to Coal Harbour: Walk along the pathway that leads from Canada Place at the end of Burrard Street to the beginning of Stanley Park, with stunning views of North Vancouver and downtown (see pages 27 and 34).

Lost Lagoon: In Stanley Park at the foot of Alberni Street. The lagoon (actually a lake) was once part of the Pacific Ocean but was cut off to accommodate the road to the Lions Gate Bridge. On its shore is the Nature House, with an aquarium, plants, library, and gift shop. Open 11am–7pm, Fri–Sun. Offers nature walks; phone (604) 257-8544 for reservations; adults $5.

Van Dusen Gardens: Situated on the grounds of a former golf course, these gardens are brilliantly maintained and beautiful throughout the year (see page 52).

Locarno and Jericho Beaches: After the Museum of Anthropology, take time for a walk on the sand from Locarno to Jericho beach and see more spectacular scenery (NW Marine Drive between Trimble and Blanca streets).

Places to Shop

Robson Street: Walk "the walk" down Robson to Denman Street; you'll find something you just have to take home.

Pacific Centre Mall: As Americans like to say, "Shop 'til you drop." With 200 stores below ground, it's easy (see page 46).

South Granville Street: Antiques, art, home furnishings, and specialty stores stretch from the south end of the Granville Bridge to 16th Street.

Views

SeaBus to Lonsdale Quay: The ride across Burrard Inlet gets you on the water quickly and easily for a view of the city from the North Shore.

Grouse Mountain: If it's a clear day or night, cross the Lions Gate Bridge to North Vancouver and take the Skyride up to Grouse. Have a drink in the bar or dinner at the Grouse Nest or just admire the city far below from the deck.

Harbour Centre Tower: Ride skylift glass elevators 553 ft (166 m) up to a 360° observation deck (admission fee); or dine in the revolving restaurant, for a spectacular view of the city and region (555 West Hastings St.; Tel. 604/689-0421).

With Kids

Vanier Park: Located just off the Burrard Street Bridge, you can stay in this corner of the city for hours visiting the lively MacMillan Space Centre, Vancouver Museum, and Maritime Museum.

Vancouver Aquarium: Even children who aren't normally enthused about heading off to see some fish will be enthralled with this excellent facility. Plus, it's in Stanley Park, so you can also visit the playground at Second Beach.

Granville Island: With the street entertainment, adventure playground, and food opportunities, everyone will have a great time (see page 44).

Further on, Lumberman's Arch sits on the site of a former Squamish village, and if you are traveling with youngsters, they'll also enjoy a detour to the **Children's Farmyard** and the **Miniature Railway**, both open daily from April to September, on weekends only from October through March.

Expansive views of North Vancouver will propel you around **Prospect Point**, the northern tip of the seawall, where seagulls grasping lunch in their beaks picnic on the rocks. Benches are plentiful if you need a place to rest or meditate. As you walk south, you'll see Siwash Rock, with its distinct lone tree standing sentry over the water. If you're hungry for a gourmet meal by this time, you'll be close to the excellent Stanley Park Teahouse at Ferguson Point (see page 138). Cross Stanley Park Drive at any point on your trek to

It's quite possible to get up-close and personal with a Steller's sea lion at Vancouver Aquarium in Stanley Park.

reach the former logging roads that now serve as trails through the forest. Chipmunks scampering down the thick tree trunks practically knock you over in their quest for an easy snack, leaving one to wonder how they manage through winter with fewer hand-outs.

Don't bypass the excellent **Vancouver Aquarium**. One of the top fish-tanks in North America and Canada's largest, it's a must-stop with or without kids. Helpful young staff members answer questions and entertain bystanders with odd insects (such as walking sticks) in the Amazon Gallery, and, if your timing is right, you might see a two-toed sloth ever-so-slowly making her way toward lunch. Massive indoor viewing tanks hold thousands of interesting and exotic species, including the arapaima, the world's largest freshwater fish. Outside, trainers discuss the beluga whales during daily exhibitions.

Just west of the aquarium are the **Rose Garden** and **Malkin Bowl**, the latter the site of **Theatre Under the Stars**, a semi-professional company that stages musical theater productions in the park on evenings from the middle of July through the middle of August.

As you head toward the Beach Street entrance to the park from the seawall, you'll pass **Second Beach**. A playground, snack bar and a new fresh water pool with a large shallow section and slides make this an irresistible spot for families. Trails from Second Beach lead to **Lost Lagoon** and its **Nature House**, which offers a research library and information on Stanley Park ecology, as well as a variety of programs, including seasonal walking tours (see page 30).

The West End and Denman Street

Don't confuse Vancouver's West End with West Vancouver (a suburb located across the Lions Gate Bridge) or with the city's West Side (a group of well-to-do neighborhoods across the Burrard Street Bridge). In fact, the **West End** is the most densely populated 194 hectares (480 acres) in Canada. Once filled with gracious homes, the area around Denman Street is now crowded with high-rise apartments and condominiums appealing to singles. In a late-1960s flurry of redevelopment, nine old houses were rescued and relocated to **Barclay Square Heritage Park**, at Nicola and Barclay streets. In particular, the 1893 **Roedde House Museum** is worth a visit to admire its displays of period clothing and furniture (guided tours only: 2 pm, Tues–Fri.)

   Denman Street itself, a nine-block strip between West Georgia Street and Beach Street dotted with countless restaurants, cafés, and shops, is a vibrant hangout—youthful, trendy, and jammed with traffic during rush hour.

DOWNTOWN VANCOUVER

No matter which downtown high-rise is casting its shadow on you, you're still only a few minutes walk from the calming sight of deep blue water: downtown Vancouver is surrounded by False Creek to the south, Burrard Inlet to the northeast, and English Bay to the west. In addition to the main commercial and waterfront districts, downtown features sightseeing areas such as Gastown and Chinatown.

The Waterfront

Water is the roadway by which a great many visitors enter Vancouver, but if you didn't arrive by ship, you can pretend otherwise with a stroll around the outer decks of **Canada Place**. Built for the 1986 World Expo, its lower levels serve as a convention center and shopping mall, with the high-rise Pan Pacific Hotel towering above all. Five famous white sails mark this spot between Howe and Hornby streets.

Though it only runs on one line, the SkyTrain is a great way to see the city, and it will get you safely to Science World.

Beyond the deck railings are unobstructed views of the North Shore, but a glance back at the brick buildings lining Gastown might prompt you to imagine Vancouver as it was 100 years ago.

Nearby on Cordova Street is the former Canadian Pacific Railway terminal, **Waterfront Station**. Rebuilt in 1914, this is the place to catch the **SeaBus** to Lonsdale Quay (see page 57) or the **SkyTrain** to Science World (see page 47). Take a look inside: the airy station is decorated with murals of the Rocky Mountains, and watching everyone bustling to and from their destinations is energizing.

> Smoking is not allowed in offices, restaurants, or inside public buildings.

Across the street from Waterfront Station is one of the city's many indoor shopping arcades, the attractive **Sinclair**

Centre. The stores here cater to healthy pocketbooks, but even window shoppers will appreciate the unhurried, open design of the building.

Robson Street and the Central Business District

Endlessly touted as the shopping mecca of Vancouver, there's a bit more to Robson Street than the fashionable hordes parading past others dining alfresco on balmy summer nights. While a portion of the street is a melange of retailers, hotels, and restaurants, once you cross Burrard Street and head east, things quiet down a bit. **Robson Square**, between Hornby and Howe streets, was designed by the acclaimed Vancouver architect Arthur Erickson. Part of a complex that includes the new provincial law courts with their sloping glass roofs, the square's public spaces entice passersby to linger. At night, a lighted waterfall provides a soothing contrast to the traffic noise. In the summer, concerts are held on the plaza, which features an outdoor ice-skating rink in winter.

The old Vancouver courthouse is now the home of the **Vancouver Art Gallery**. A fine example of Classical architecture, the gallery features a floor dedicated to the paintings of Emily Carr, a native of Victoria and one of western Canada's most celebrated artists and writers.

Farther down Robson between Homer and Hamilton streets, the relatively new **Library Square** is an awe-inspiring sight. Reminiscent of a Roman coliseum from the outside, the inside is pure fun, with small shops and coffee outlets partially ringing the entrance to the public library's stacks. Across Homer is the **Centre in Vancouver for the Performing Arts**, home to traveling musicals and a gift shop selling theater-oriented trinkets, T-shirts, and books.

The verdigris roof of **The Fairmont Hotel Vancouver** on West Georgia and Burrard streets is almost as symbolic of the city as Stanley Park. This is the third incarnation of the hotel, the first having opened in 1887 and rebuilt in 1916 on Granville and Georgia streets, currently the site of Sear's department store. Construction on the present hotel began in 1928 but wasn't completed until 1939, opening in time to greet King George VI of England. Along with its status as a landmark, the hotel is host to a number of exclusive shops.

Christ Church Cathedral now shares Cathedral Place with the Canadian Craft Museum.

Continuing a bit down Burrard Street, you come to **Christ Church Cathedral**, an Anglican parish church completed in 1895. After escaping from the threat of demolition in the 1970s, the sandstone building became part of lofty **Cathedral Place**, built in 1991, which also houses the **Canadian Craft Museum**. This diminutive and lovely two-story gallery displays ceramics, textiles, glass, and jewelry by artists throughout Canada. Be sure to notice the glorious Art Deco stained-glass door at the back of the museum, a relic from the building this complex replaced.

Art Deco aficionados will also appreciate the **Marine Building** at Hastings and Burrard, a masterwork of detail and, with 25 stories, once the tallest building in the province of British Columbia. Be sure to enter the lobby to admire the stained glass and murals (1929–1930) depicting Vancouver's maritime history.

Gastown

Vancouver's history as a city began in **Gastown**, yet these 2½ hectares (6 acres) were left to languish for decades until community groups and property owners began drawing attention to the area's importance and possibilities. In 1971 Gastown was declared a heritage district, and the following year the federal and provincial governments helped the city pay for renovations that included Victorian-style lamp posts, red brick streets, and greenery.

Ostensibly designed to attract tourists, an unfortunate number of knickknack shops now dominate the landscape

The old Vancouver courthouse is now the stately residence of the Vancouver Art Gallery.

and overwhelm the historical aspects of the neighborhood. Nonetheless, visitors seem universally delighted to catch sight of the **Steam Clock** on the corner of Cambie and Water streets. Constructed in 1977 based on an older design, the clock whistles in 15-minute intervals and blows steam on the hour. Two blocks down at Carrall and Water is Maple Tree Square, presided over appropriately by a bronze statue of **John Deighton**, the legendary "Gassy Jack," who supplied whiskey to Vancouver's fledgling populace and was most likely the source of the district's name. June through August, free 90-minute guided walking tours are given by the **Gastown Improvement Society**, leaving from Maple Tree Square at 2pm (Tel.: 604/683-5650).

Don't be afraid to cross the street at designated crosswalks. Vancouver drivers really do stop for pedestrians.

If you're planning to cross Gastown into Chinatown on foot, head south on Carrall to East Pender to avoid the worst of the city's skid row on East Hastings Street.

Chinatown

Chinese arrived in Vancouver to work on the railroads, and North America's third largest **Chinatown** has a history dating back to 1858. In the once thriving community of Richmond, a generation of old-timers has died out and made room for the Asian immigrants who have flocked to the suburb, where behemoth concrete shopping malls have replaced the crowded stores lining Pender Street as the place to purchase life's essentials. Commerce in today's Chinatown is nevertheless alive and well, as evidenced by the crowds at the night market on Keefer and Main streets, open from May through September from 6:30pm to 11:30pm every Friday, Saturday, and Sunday.

While poking around the stores and admiring the architecture, stop to gawk at the world's skinniest insurance office, the 2-m- (6-ft-) wide **Sam Kee Building** on Pender and Carrall streets. Built in 1913, it's a staple of the *Ripley's Believe It or Not* books. The **Chinese Cultural Centre** (50 East Pender Street), built in 1981, is a community resource that hosts Chinese opera and dance events as well as classes and holiday celebrations. The building is fronted by a traditional gateway constructed in China for Expo '86 and a second celebratory gate nearby opened in 2002.

On Carrall at Keefer Street, behind the Chinese Cultural Centre, is the **Dr. Sun Yat-Sen Classical Garden**, a Ming Dynasty-style jewel constructed by artisans from China without a single nail or screw. Volunteer docents add immeasurably to a tour of the garden by describing how Chinese stories and culture influenced the placement of each rock, tree, and gate. Try timing your arrival to coincide with a tour —it's an hour well spent.

FALSE CREEK AND GRANVILLE ISLAND

Until the mid-1850s, the wayward tributary of English Bay called **False Creek** provided generations of Squamish natives with a living in the form of fish and wildlife. The industrialization of the shores of False Creek began with lumber mills in the 1860s and continued until the end of World War II, when a combination of troubles (including pollution and factory closures) led to suggestions that the creek be drained. As yet another example of local politics and luck conspiring to benefit the city, False Creek instead became a model of urban renewal.

The Chinese Cultural Center is a valuable community resource for North America's third-largest Chinatown.

Museums and Galleries

BC Sports Hall of Fame and Museum. *777* Pacific Boulevard; Tel. (604) 687-5520. 10am–5pm; adults $6, seniors/students $4, children under 5 free.

Canadian Craft Museum. 639 Hornby Street; Tel. (604) 687-8266. Mon–Sat 10am–5pm, Thur to 9pm, Sun 12–5pm, closed Tue 30 Sept–1 May; adults $5, students/seniors $3, children under 12 free, free to all Thur 5–9pm.

MacMillan Space Centre. Vanier Park, 1100 Chestnut Street; Tel. (604) 738-7827. Tue–Sun 10am–5pm (daily Jul–Aug); adult $12.75, senior/youth 11–18 $9.75, children 5–10 $8.75, children under 5 free (but including "Virtual Voyage" $5.25), family (2 adults plus up to 3 children) $40.

Museum of Anthropology. 6393 Northwest Marine Drive; Tel. (604) 822-5087. Wed–Sun 10am–5pm, Tue to 9pm, closed Mon, 8 Sept–24 May; adults $7, seniors $5, students $4, children under 6 free, family (2 adults plus up to 4 children under 18) $20, free Tuesday evenings.

Old Hastings Mill Store Museum. 1575 Alma Road; Tel. (604) 734-1212. Daily in summer, weekends in winter; free.

Roedde House Museum. 1415 Barclay Street; Tel. (604) 684-7040. Call for a schedule. Guided tours Tue–Fri at 2pm.

Vancouver Aquarium. Stanley Park; Tel. (604) 685-3364. Daily 10am–5:30pm, summer 9:30am–7pm; adults $13.85, youth 13–18/students/seniors $11.70, children 4–12 $9.15, children under 4 free; family (2 adults/3 children) $45.95.

Vancouver Art Gallery. 750 Hornby Street; Tel. (604) 662-4700. Mon–Fri 10am–5:30pm, Thur to 9pm, Sat 10am–5;30 pm, Sun 12–5pm; adults $12.50, seniors $7, students $5.50, free for children 12 and under; Thur 5–9pm $4 min donation.

Vancouver Maritime Museum. 1905 Ogden Avenue; Tel. (604) 257-8300. Tue–Sat 10am–5pm, Sun 12–5pm; adults $7, students/seniors $4, family (2 adults plus 2 children) $16.

Vancouver Museum. Vanier Park, 1100 Chestnut Street; Tel. (604) 736-4431. Open daily 10am–5pm, Thur to 9pm; adults $8, seniors $7, youth (under 19) $5.50.

Gulf of Georgia Cannery Museum. 12138 4th Avenue (in Steveston); Tel. (604) 664-9009. Thur–Mon 10am–5pm (June 1–Sept 3 daily 10am–5pm); adults $6.50, seniors/students $5, youth 6–16 $3.25, family: $16.25.

Gardens and Parks

Bloedel Floral Conservatory. Queen Elizabeth Park, 33rd Avenue at Cambie Street; Tel. (604) 257-8596. Daily 10am–5pm; adults $3.25, seniors $2, youth 6–18 $1.60, children under 6 free.

Nitobe Memorial Garden. University of British Columbia campus; Tel. (604) 822-6038. Summer 10am–6pm, limited hours fall–winter; adults $2.75, seniors/students $1.75, youth 6–13 $1.50, children under 6 free.

Dr. Sun-Yat-Sen Classical Chinese Gardens. 578 Carrall Street; Tel. (604) 662-3207. Spring 10am–6pm, summer 9:30am–7pm, autumn/winter 10am–4:30pm; adults $7.50, seniors $6, students $5, children under 5 free.

University of British Columbia Botanical Garden. 6804 Southwest Marine Dr; Tel. (604) 822-4186. Spring–summer 10am–6pm, until 5pm fall–winter; adults $4.75, seniors/students $2.50, children 6–13 $2, under 6 free.

VanDusen Botanical Gardens Association. 5251 Oak Street; Tel. (604) 878-9274. Restaurant/gift shop. Open 10am daily, closes at 4pm Oct–Mar, 6pm Apr, 8 or 9pm May–Sept; adults $6.50, seniors $4, children 6-12 $3.25, youth 13-18 $5, under 6 free, family pass $15.

Lynn Canyon Ecology Centre. 3663 Park Road, North Vancouver; Tel. (604) 981-3103. Daily 7am–7pm, spring and fall until 8pm, summer 9pm; Ecology Centre open daily 10am–5pm; Dec and Jan closed weekends & holidays; free.

Lower Seymour Conservation Reserve. At north end of Lillooet Road, North Vancouver District; Tel. (604) 987-1273 for tour and general information. Daily 8am–9pm summer, until 5pm rest of year; free.

Granville Island

The star of the False Creek redevelopment story is most definitely **Granville Island**. It's not an island at all, actually, just a mushroom-shaped piece of land jutting out into the water, accessible by car from the **Granville Bridge** and by ferry from Science World, Yaletown, and the Hornby Street Pier. Reclaimed from industrial doom in 1979, the "island" is a self-contained village crowned by the colorful, noisy, and crowded **Granville Island Public Market**. Stall after stall displays fruits and vegetables, bakery goods, meats, fish, gifts, candy, and flowers—a bountiful source for cooks and eaters.

Outside the market there's usually a full schedule of entertaining street performers, and nearby is the justly popular **Kids Only Market**: a massive collection of toys, books, games, clothing, and candy. Adults are more than welcome to help the little ones shop (after all, we know who's holding the credit cards), but beware of the video and arcade games on the second floor, from which you might not escape until closing time.

Former industrial buildings with corrugated roofs also shelter arts and crafts galleries, studios, offices, and even an art school named after Emily Carr. The Granville Island Hotel provides cheery lodgings, and a variety of restaurants overlook the bridges, water, and sea-faring activity. Granville Island is a popular night spot, too. The **Arts Club Theatre** produces shows throughout the year, and its Backstage Lounge presents a regular roster of musicians.

Be forewarned that parking, especially on weekends, is difficult, as is maneuvering a car through the narrow streets. You can easily take the bus to Granville Island, or leave your car on Pacific Avenue near Hornby Street and ride the little **AquaBus** across False Creek.

Yaletown

The southeast edge of False Creek is currently undergoing development into a new residential community. But a small nearby area between Nelson and Davie streets has already metamorphosed into a hip and happening district. **Yaletown** (or "Yaletown High," as some of its residents flippantly call it, referring to its small-town, everyone-knows-everyone feeling) is filled with interesting boutiques, restaurants, and clubs. Although it's only two blocks long and two blocks wide, you can easily let an afternoon slip away going from one shop to another with a break for drinks or a meal.

The **BC Sports Hall of Fame and Museum**, is located at Gate A of **BC Place Stadium**. The stadium is covered by the world's biggest air-supported dome; it hosts concerts and

Take a guided tour through Chinatown's Dr. Sun-Yat-Sen Classical Garden, one of Vancouver's undisputed gems.

What If It's Raining?

A true Vancouverite never lets a little precipitation get in the way of a good time. Nevertheless, a short list of umbrella-free activities is always useful in an unpredictable climate.

Shopping. The underground **Pacific Centre Mall** at West Georgia and Granville extends to Dunsmuir Street, with entrances through the department stores anchoring the corners. If the 200 or so shops here don't wear you out, hop on the **SkyTrain** at the Granville stop under The Bay (a department store) to the Metrotown station in Burnaby. There you'll discover more stores in two malls connected by a pedestrian bridge, and you won't even get your feet wet.

High Tea. Hotel dining might not be your cup of java, but for elegance and service, there's no finer place to go for afternoon tea, especially on a cold, wet day. Try Fleuri at the Sutton Place Hotel for either a classic English tea or, for a more cultural experience, a traditional Japanese tea. The Fairmont Hotel Vancouver also serves a lovely afternoon tea in the Lobby Lounge.

Pampering. Nineteen day spas provide enough services to keep you relaxed and very happy until the clouds subside. Downtown, investigate the holistic, wellness, beauty and anti-aging treatments at La Raffinage (Tel. 604/681-9933) or check out the massages and wraps at Versailles Spa (Tel. 604/732-7865). Among others, Waterfront Centre, Sutton Place, and Fairmont Hotel Vancouver offer spa sevices.

Culture. Take advantage of the weather by prolonging a visit to UBC's Museum of Anthropology. Don't rush away after the docent tour, but take some time to look around the Koerner Ceramics Gallery and peruse the many see-through drawers housing First Nation's relics.

exhibitions as well as the BC Lions football team. Dedicated sports fans should pop into the museum for a tour of British Columbia's sports history. Hands-on exhibits allow twitching muscles to get some exercise.

At the very end of False Creek is **Science World** (Tel. 604/443-7443), with its distinctive silver-colored dome also dating from Expo '86. This hands-on, interactive science museum appeals to both little and big kids with a host of permanent and changing exhibits on natural phenomena. The top floor features an Omnimax theater (hence the dome), showing documentary films, such as Everest, on an enormous screen with a wrap-around sound system. If it's raining, this is an excellent place to entertain the children.

THE WEST SIDE AND THE EAST SIDE

From downtown, the Burrard Street and Granville Street bridges cross False Creek and lead to Vancouver's **West Side**, a series of neighborhoods ranging from tony Shaughnessy Heights, whose early residents were the cream of Vancouver society in the 1920s, to perky Kitsilano, where 1960s bohemians have morphed into the present day bourgeoisie. A number of worthwhile attractions and pleasant beaches are located on the West Side, not to mention some of the city's most vaunted restaurants.

Kitsilano

Named for Squamish Chief Khahtsahlanough in 1905, **Kitsilano** is a popular neighborhood with young, well-to-do families. The main shopping district, Kits, lies on West 4th Street: a terrific collection of home décor, clothing, sporting goods, and health food shops interspersed with a variety of ethnic and high-end restaurants and new residential condos and flats.

The Vancouver Maritime Museum in Vanier Park provides plenty of seaworthy sights for sailors of all ages.

Vanier Park, which was a Native settlement in the latter half of the 19th century, lies on the shores of English Bay and is accessible off the first Burrard Street Bridge exit. Among the park's charms are the well-designed and interesting Vancouver Museum and the MacMillan Space Centre.

The **Vancouver Museum** takes you through several thousand years of local history in an accessible and entertaining manner that will appeal to kids and adults. Start with an Egyptian mummy of a boy collected by a 19th-century Vancouver doctor. Then proceed to the deck of a sailing ship, a Hudson's Bay Company frontier trading post, an 1880s Railway car, fancy Victorian and Edwardian parlors, and a unique exhibit of 1940s and 1950s neon signs, relics of the city's days as the West's glitziest metropolis.

The **MacMillan Space Centre** shares the premises with the museum. Formerly the H. R. MacMillan Planetarium, it is now modernized and renamed to appeal to 21st-century travelers. There are many intriguing activities at the Space Centre, but if you are shepherding children, be sure to pur-

chase the admission package that includes a ride on the Mars simulator and one of the clever multimedia shows on the solar system in the second floor theater.

Also in Vanier Park visit the **Vancouver Maritime Museum**, with ship models, photographs, and a children's interactive exhibit called the "Maritime Discovery Centre." Walk on the Heritage Harbour docks to admire the vintage boats and take in the views. During the summer months,

This sculpture by Bill Reid takes center stage at the Museum of Anthropology.

Shakespeare gets his due here through "Bard at the Beach," a series of productions staged in a tent overlooking the bay.

A walking and cycling path will lead you to **Kitsilano Beach Park** between Trafalgar and Maple streets. It features an outdoor salt-water pool, tennis courts, and an opportunity to admire all the healthy young locals on their days off.

The 1886 fire that destroyed Gastown spared few buildings, but one that survives to this day now graces **Pioneer Park** in Point Grey at the end of Alma Street. The **Hastings Mill Store** dates from 1865 and serves as a catch-all museum of relics including an embroidered portrait of **Queen Victoria**. Nearby, **Jericho Beach Park**, a former military base, is the site of the annual **Vancouver Folk Festival**, held the third weekend in July. A youth hostel is located in former barracks overlooking the water.

Point Grey and the University of British Columbia

The exclusive **Point Grey** neighborhood encompasses two of Vancouver's best beaches, Locarno and Spanish Banks, and the vast campus of the **University of British Columbia** (UBC). Although land for the new university was endowed in 1911 by the government and UBC opened in 1915, classes weren't held at the Point Grey site until 1925.

As you head toward the campus on West 4th (which becomes Chancellor Boulevard), you'll notice a great tract of forest. The university had originally intended to develop much of this land for housing, leaving only a small portion of the area's old-growth woodland for a park. A series of unforeseen circumstances conspired to delay the parceling off of lots, including transportation difficulties, the Great Depression, shortages during World War II, and, in the 1960s and 1970s, community resistance. As a result, the university's plan to destroy the forest never came to fruition. Instead, the 763-hectare (1,885-acre) **Pacific Spirit Regional Park** was officially established in 1988. Its 55 km (34 miles) of trails are open to the public for hiking, biking, and horseback riding—although there really isn't anywhere nearby to procure a horse.

Once inside university grounds, you'll pass the **Chan Centre for the Performing Arts** (Tel. 604/822-2697). These state-of-the-art facilities include a 1,400-seat concert hall with stellar acoustics, a 250-seat studio theater, and a 160-seat cinema. There's a free tour of the facility offered on Tuesdays and Fridays at 1pm. A schedule of recitals, contemporary and classic plays, and other events can be seen on the Centre's web site, http://www.chancentre.com.

It might be stretching a point to say that Arthur Erickson is to modern architecture in Vancouver as Antonio Gaudí is to Modernist architecture in Barcelona. Nevertheless, UBC's **Museum of Anthropology** is one of Erickson's most admired structures. Built in 1976 on a bluff overlooking English Bay, the museum is a 20th-century rendition of a First Nations longhouse (ceremonial building) with superb natural lighting and a far-ranging collection of West Coast Native art. Docents lead an hour-long tour of the main gallery, providing interesting background on the displays that conclude with the famous carving *The Raven and the First Men*, by Haida artist Bill Reid. Leave time for private exploration after the tour, for the majority of the museum's collections are cleverly displayed in easily accessible glass-topped drawers. And don't miss the **Koerner Ceramics Gallery** at the west end of the building. It contains thousands of contemporary Canadian and European works but is often overlooked by museum visitors.

Across the street and a short walk away (marked by a small, easy-to-miss sign) is the **Nitobe Memorial Garden**. The small, attractive, and carefully maintained garden features man-made waterfalls, a pond, and a teahouse among the trees and shrubs. The university also cultivates the 28-hectare (69-acre) **UBC Botanical Gardens**, divided into five distinct green belts: the British Columbia Native Garden, Asian Garden, Physick Garden, Alpine Garden, and Food Garden. The layout can seem confusing, so ask for a map at the entrance. The gardens are best visited in the spring or summer when the plants are still blooming.

Shaughnessy and Little Mountain

Located on the old Shaughnessy Golf Course about a 15-minute drive from downtown, the **Van Dusen Botanical Gardens** are a year-round glory. This city-owned, nonprofit Eden comprises 22 hectares (59 acres) of theme gardens and a delightfully tricky labyrinth hedge maze. The multitude of plants along the many paths are all identified, and the park is well-signed and easy to navigate. It's one of the prettiest botanical gardens around. If you happen to be visiting during

---

Barely There

The human form, in all its glory, gets its due at the bottom of the cliffs below the UBC law school (not far from the Museum of Anthropology). That's where you'll find **Wreck Beach**, Vancouver's sole clothing-optional spot for summer sun worshipers. Vendors wearing little more than aprons to serve as cash registers supply the many thousands of beach-goers with food, drink, and decorative items. Self-righteous sermonizers occasionally make the steep trek down to the sand to preach hellfire and damnation—weather permitting, of course.

A vast expanse of plant life awaits at the perennially exquisite Van Dusen Botanical Gardens.

the fall, you'll be dazzled by the colors of the turning leaves. The gift shop is full of appealing items for horticulturists, and there is a full-service restaurant (Shaughnessy) serving lunch and dinner daily in the shop pavilion.

A bit farther east is **Queen Elizabeth Park** (also known as "Little Mountain"), on Cambie Street at 33rd. A former rock quarry, this park marks the high ground as well as the geographical center of Vancouver. It's a favorite site for wedding photographs; on summer Saturdays you'll no doubt see many a bride traipsing up one of the paths. Along with Seasons in the Park, a restaurant that hosted Boris Yeltsin and Bill Clinton during their 1993 summit, the **Bloedel** **Conservatory** shares the Little Mountain summit and is open year round. Tropical birds fly freely amid the conservatory's rainforest-like setting, which shelters unusual plants collected from all over the world.

At the foot of the mountain on Ontario Street is a charming 6,500-seat baseball park called **Nat Bailey Stadium**. Baseball fans can attend summer home games of the Canadians, Vancouver's Triple-A Pacific Coast League baseball team (see page 91).

The East Side: Commercial Drive

The Grandview neighborhood on the East Side of Vancouver is referred to as **"Little Italy,"** but it has traditionally sheltered a diverse working-class population. Just 10 minutes by car from downtown (or take the SkyTrain to the Broadway

The Bloedel Conservatory at Queen Elizabeth Park hosts tropical flora and fauna.

Station), it is one of Vancouver's more affordable areas (a vanishing breed), with young families increasingly arriving and renovating the pre-World War I homes. The shopping district, centered on **Commercial Drive**, truly reflects both the city's cross-cultural mix and a marvelous vitality. It's one of the areas where you'll see evidence of Vancouver family life —lots of baby strollers and fathers leading toddlers past the open-air produce markets—and it's apparently where the counterculture goes for coffee. A great place to take in the scene is from a table at Havana (see page 137). Then, meander down the street, perhaps collecting a picnic lunch from the local Italian deli or snacks from one of the many bakeries. For dinner, try Dario's in the Italian Cultural Centre.

EXCURSIONS

Day trips beyond the city limits can be as close as a 20-minute drive across the Lions Gate Bridge to North or West Vancouver, or as far as a 12- to 14-hour round-trip to Victoria for those folks determined to sip a cup of tea in the genteel surroundings of the Empress Hotel. The mountains from the North Shore to Whistler offer wintertime skiing opportunities and summertime hiking, and vast regional parks are also awash with trails and gorgeous scenery. Hopping on a ferry to one of the islands is another only-in-Vancouver activity, one that can be a vacation in itself if you have a few days to spare.

North Vancouver

The shores of **North Vancouver** were the exclusive long-time home of First Nations people until 1862, when a couple of businessmen decided to build a sawmill east of what became the northern end of the Lions Gate Bridge. It was another three decades before the District of North Vancouver

The Capilano Suspension Bridge is considered North Vancouver's very first tourist attraction.

managed to incorporate, and at the time there were only a few hundred non-Native residents scattered about the area. Even then, entrepreneurs provided "ferry" transportation across Burrard Inlet (a rowboat, actually). One pioneering Scotsman, George Grant MacKay, inadvertently built the area's first tourist attraction, the Capilano Suspension Bridge. With the completion of the **Lions Gate Bridge** in 1938 and the **Second Narrows Bridge** in 1960 (the latter is east of Vancouver and part of the TransCanada Highway), and the availability of speedy SeaBus service between the shores, North Vancouver has become a bedroom community for the metropolis across the inlet.

Today, North Vancouver is actually divided into two separate municipalities, **North Vancouver District** and **North Vancouver City**; the latter was incorporated in 1907. North "Van" City took the bulk of the spoils when it split off from the District, annexing Grouse Mountain and Lynn Canyon Park. The District, however, encompasses **Seymour Provincial Park**, another fine area for hiking.

The SeaBus leaves from downtown Vancouver's Waterfront Station every 15 minutes for a short but sweet 12-minute scenic ride across Burrard Inlet to **Lonsdale Quay**. Another boon of Expo '86, Lonsdale Quay is a smaller, less hectic, and more compact version of the Granville Island Public Market. Along with a hotel, there are gift shops, boutiques, restaurants, and a full range of fresh goodies to purchase at individual stalls inside the first-floor market.

Lynn Canyon Park

To the west of the ferry dock and behind the market is a bus terminal with connections to **Lynn Canyon Park**, among other destinations. Two bus lines wind through residential neighborhoods up to the canyon (the number 229 bus stops almost at the entrance), so there's no real need to drive. The 250-hectare (618-acre) forest offers 161 km (100 miles) of hiking trails through dense pines; the only sounds you'll hear

(besides other hikers) are birds and water running through the rocks. A small ecology center on the main road offers an introduction to forestry, Canadian-style. Lynn Canyon also has its own suspension bridge, a little shorter than the more famous Capilano attraction, but free and just as nerve-wracking. This is the place to test your fear of heights without first making any monetary investment.

Seymour Provincial Park

Hikers will be delighted to discover the **Lower Seymour Conservation Reserve**, which opened to the public in 1987. Located in North Vancouver District at the north end of Lillooet Road (cross the Second Narrows Bridge; exit at Capilano College/Lillooet Road and continue past the cemetery), the site was developed to illustrate forest sustainability and resource management. These are important issues for British Columbia, where approximately 60 percent of the economy depends on this natural resource. At 5,200 hectares (12,849 acres), Seymour is nearly 13 times as large as Stanley Park. On the weekends, skaters and bicyclists share the 11-km (7-mile) gravel road to **Seymour Falls Dam** along with the foot traffic, but the path is restricted to hikers only during the week before 5pm. Vehicular traffic is excluded. **Rice Lake** is stocked with trout (fishing licenses are required for adults), and there is an easy walking trail around it that is wheelchair accessible. During salmon-spawning season, be sure to drive or take the park's shuttle bus to the **Seymour Salmonid Hatchery**. It's fascinating to glimpse part of the salmon's life-cycle play itself out. On summer Sundays there are free guided walks as well as bus tours.

In North Vancouver, Lynn Canyon Park is the ideal place to experience unspoiled nature and all its tranquil beauty.

Grouse Mountain

A tired-but-true Vancouver cliché informs us that, given the right season, in this locale it's possible to ski in the morning and swim in the afternoon. **Grouse Mountain**, a 15-minute drive from the city over the Lions Gate Bridge, provides the skiing in this equation, but it's even a popular stop after the

First Nations

First Nations peoples are surprisingly under-represented when it comes to visitor attractions in Vancouver. Totem poles can be spotted in many tourist sites and parks, but with the exception of the Museum of Anthropology (see page 51), there are few places to gather significant details about the culture and history of the Northwest Coast Natives. While the museum's collection is unique and potent, it still leaves the impression of Native culture as belonging to the past.

Happily, the addition on Grouse Mountain of the **Hiwus Feasthouse** helps fill the breach between past and present with an entertaining multimedia program of native food, stories, song, and dance. The evening begins at the Grouse Mountain Lodge, where you meet your guide for an easy hike to the cedar longhouse. Guests are then seated on cushioned chiefs' benches. Between dances and legends performed by local members of the Salish and Musqueam tribes, a multi-course dinner is served in cedar boxes and baskets. The program ends with the audience participating in a rousing ceremonial dance—one sure way to develop a relationship among cultures. For ticket information, phone Grouse Mountain Guest Services at (604) 980-9311. Currently, the Hiwus Feasthouse is open to the public from May to early October.

snow has melted. Once you reach the foot of the mountain, there are two ways to get to the top: one is scenic, one strenuous. The **Grouse Mountain Skyride**, an aerial tram that whisks passengers 1,100 m (3,609 ft) over the treetops, provides the views. It leaves every 15 minutes from 9am until midnight daily. The more difficult and considerably longer trip up to the resort area is a challenging 3-km (2-mile) hike called the **Grouse Grind**. Uphill all the way, this is not a walk for the faint-of-heart or out-of-shape hiker. Staff in the information center can direct you to the trailhead. At the summit there are still

During the summer, you can take a free tour of the 1912 Point Atkinson Lighthouse.

more hiking trails, a children's playground, a lodge with two restaurants, gift shops, and a movie theater, in addition to the ski lift, which operates all year. Besides skiing, winter activities include sleigh rides, ice skating, snowshoeing, and snow-boarding. Thrill seekers can paraglide in the summer or join a mountain bike tour down Grouse.

On your way up to Grouse Mountain, you'll pass billboards advertising the **Capilano Suspension Bridge** and **Capilano Park**. The 137-m (450-ft) cedar bridge, in one variation or another, has been attracting customers almost since its inception in 1889 and rates as the area's oldest amusement. There is no doubt about the purpose of this attraction: it is designed to part excited people from their dollars. But it's well-designed and immensely appealing, especially to kids. The bridge isn't the area's sole draw, as it is surrounded by a nature park with trails and a trout pond, a carving exhibition, fast food counters, and one of the largest gift shops you'll ever see. Expect crowds during the high season, as this is one sure stop on every tourbus schedule.

West Vancouver

If you veer left off the Lions Gate (First Narrows) Bridge onto Marine Drive, you'll discover **West Vancouver**, a residential community with a reputation for high per capita income. That is not the area's only claim to fame, however. It is also home to Canada's first shopping mall, **the Park Royal**, which was constructed in 1950. "West Van" also sports a seawall promenade like its neighbor across the inlet, but with a twist—here there is a separate sidewalk for dogs. You can reach the seawall from the delightful **Ambleside Park** (Marine Drive to 13th Street). There are also some terrific restaurants and good shopping along Marine Drive.

Continue north on Marine Drive and watch carefully for the turn into **Lighthouse Park**. If you're lucky enough to arrive in the off-season or during a workday, you might be treated to a blissfully private walk among old-growth Douglas firs inside this 75-hectare (185-acre) forest. The briefest hike, an easy 10 minutes on the main road, ends at the picturesque **Point Atkinson Lighthouse**, completed in 1912 to replace the 1870s-era original structure. The lighthouse is staffed, with free tours available for the asking in the summer.

Travelers can reach the town of **Horseshoe Bay** by riding the bus through West Vancouver. If you aren't planning to take the ferry to Bowen Island, Langdale, or Nanaimo, it's quite pleasant to wander the docks at Horseshoe Bay and watch the boats in Howe Sound. (If you are driving and in a hurry to catch a ferry, be sure to follow the signs to Highway 99; if you take the detour through West Vancouver, you will spend double the time.)

Bowen Island

The closest port from Horseshoe Bay is **Snug Cove** on **Bowen Island**, a 20-minute trip by ferry. Nicknamed the "Happy Isle" by its promoters 70 years ago, Bowen was the scene of summer picnics and dances in the 1930s enjoyed by

Snug Cove's marina is always busy with sailors from Vancouver, disembarking for sojourns on Bowen Island.

Mountain bikers crowd the slopes during summer on Whistler Mountain, a skier's delight in winter.

hundreds of mainlanders who cruised over for an evening's entertainment. Today, many Vancouver sailors dock their craft in the harbor and others have moved to the island year-round to enjoy small-town life and a relatively short commute to the city.

Bowen consists of a minuscule but sophisticated shopping area above the docks on the main road with a few restaurants, a bakery, a bookstore, gift and clothing shops, and a gallery. Among the activities to pursue here is hiking in **Crippen Regional Park**, on 259 hectares (640 acres) of land once controlled by the Union Steamship Company. The company's old general store on the site is now a community center. Two public beaches and a lake are accessible by car, and there are a fair number of bed-and-breakfasts on the island should you be so charmed that you'd rather not leave. An especially lovely and invigorating way to enjoy a few hours is kayaking around **Howe Sound**, looking up at the geese or down at the salmon. Bowen Island Sea Kayaking rents the equipment you'll need from an office on the docks and offers the option of a guided tour or lessons (see page 90). Equally wonderful is leaving the car at Horseshoe Bay, walking onto the ferry for a late-afternoon crossing, and having dinner at the Beggar's Purse (be sure to make reservations; see page 141) before taking the last boat back to Vancouver at 9pm: a very romantic evening!

Whistler

Skiers recognize the name **Whistler** immediately and without further explanation. Arguably the premier ski resort in North America, its chalet-style hotels, chalet-style lodges, chalet-style condominium developments, and chalet-style pedestrian-only outdoor shopping center resemble an illustrated fairytale: "Once upon a time, there was a village invented solely for the pursuit of leisure activities..."

It's a story that ends happily ever after, if the numbers of vacationers are any indication. More than two million arrive from all over the world in the winter to ski down Whistler and Blackcomb Mountains, to snowboard, to tramp through the forest on snowshoes, even to fish. In summer the paths around Whistler's five lakes are filled with walkers and bicyclists, while the ski lifts allow hikers to begin their treks at high elevations and work their way down the mountain. Golf attracts many an enthusiast to four world-renowned courses around the valley, and tennis players have their pick of resort or public courts. Horseback riding is another option; there are small stables in Whistler itself, but for a really magnificent ride you can trot to one of the stables in Pemberton, 35 km (28 miles) north of town.

Even people looking to relax in less strenuous ways can design a perfect vacation. **Whistler Village** is filled with shops and restaurants, and most of the resort hotels have full-service health spas, swimming pools, Jacuzzis, video game rooms, and other indoor amenities. There's also a public recreation center, the **Meadow Park Sports Centre** (Tel. 604/935-8350). For a reasonable fee, visitors have access to the indoor swimming pools, sauna, steam room, squash courts, fitness center, and ice skating rink.

Certainly the journey to Whistler will be a memorable experience in itself. Depending on weather and traffic, the drive from Vancouver takes about two hours on Highway 99, the spectacular "Sea to Sky" route that hugs the coast as you climb toward the mountains. Take advantage of the many roadside stops in provincial parks, which feature small lakes, beautiful creeks, streams, and cliffs where rock climbers hone their technique. **Shannon Falls** is a particularly photo-worthy detour, with a dramatic waterfall within sight of the parking lot. Once you pass Squamish, don't be misled by the signs indicating your arrival in Whistler. Like many winter resort towns, the road to Whistler is bordered by clumps of condos spread for several miles along the highway. Whistler Village is situated behind one of the last clusters, surrounded on one end by parking lots.

If you aren't driving, you have several other options to reach the mountain. Maverick Coach Lines (Tel. 604/ 940-2332) departs six times a day from the Vancouver bus depot at Main and Terminal streets. Perimeter's Whistler Express (Tel. toll free 877/317-7788) leaves from the

Vancouver Airport for the three-hour ride to Whistler seven to eleven times daily, depending on the season. You can also charter a helicopter, hire a limousine, or even take the train. BC Rail (Tel. 604/984-5246 or toll-free 800-663-8238) chugs along daily between North Vancouver and Whistler; reasonable one-way adult fares include breakfast on the 7am morning run and dinner on the 6:10pm evening return. The ride takes approximately 2½ hours, and there is a free connecting bus service into Whistler Village from the train station.

The area boasts a number of fine restaurants and hotels. Certainly the most lavishly praised is the luxurious Fairmont **Chateau Whistler Resort** at the base of Blackcomb Mountain. It's quite a site, nearly as imposing as the mountain itself, and if you don't happen to be staying there, be sure to stop in anyway to look around or have a drink. The Village bursts with a number of high-line ski and sportswear stores, and standbys such as Gap, Levi's, and the ubiquitous Starbucks.

The town operates a well-oiled tourism call center, where friendly operators will assist you with lodging reservations. Dial 800-944-7853 (toll free) in Canada and the US, (604) 664-5625 elsewhere (website: www.tourismwhistler.com). For just about everything else, the **Whistler Activity and Information Centre** at the Whistler Conference Centre (same toll free number, or 604/932-2394) can help you make plans.

Steveston

This quaint fishing village on the edge of the Fraser River's south arm is awash in history. About a 30-minute drive from downtown Vancouver, **Steveston** is the largest commercial fishing port in Canada. But from the late 1890s until World

Shannon Falls is one of the spectacular photogenic sights along the "Sea to Sky" route to Whistler.

War II, it was also the thriving center of the canning business. To gain some understanding of the importance of the fishing industry in British Columbia and how it affected the lives of the local population—once primarily Japanese—start your tour at the **Gulf of Georgia Cannery** (see page 43 for hours). The biggest operation in Steveston's heyday, it's now a protected Heritage site with exhibits on the history of West Coast fishing, including a short film, a children's activity area, and a fascinating scale model of the canning process from fish to finish.

The tiny **Steveston Museum** and Post Office on Moncton Street, in a 1906 prefabricated structure that once housed a bank, presents a bit of turn-of-the-century life and some photographs of the once rowdy town. The museum is open daily to the public for self-guided tours. A bit farther east at the end of Railway Avenue is the **Britannia Heritage Shipyard,** a working shipyard where you can watch wooden boats being repaired and built.

A new attraction in Steveston is offered May to October by Vancouver Whale Watch (Tel. 604-274-9565). Speedy Zodiac craft take you among the Gulf Islands in Georgia Bay to spot the orcas, porpoises, sea lions, and bald eagles. A professional naturalist leads the way, armed with a hydrophone—so you can listen to the animals underwater. They also operate a more leisurely 35-minute guided tour of the Steveston Harbour on the *River Queen.*

Be sure and sample the fish and chips, sold by competing eateries around **Steveston Landing** on Bayview Street, as well as on the *River Queen.* A full day in the Steveston area must include a hike or ride on the paths through **Garry Point Park** along the shore. Rent bikes at Steveston Bicycle on Chatham Street (Tel. 604/271-5544.)

The Gulf of Georgia Cannery provides an interesting historical perspective within the quaint village of Steveston.

Victoria: An Abbreviated History

1790 Spanish explorer Manuel Quimper claims west coast of island for Spain.

1842 James Douglas selects Victoria as new site for Hudson's Bay Company post.

1843 Fort construction begins on 4 June on the site of today's Bastion Square.

1849 Britain leases Vancouver Island to Hudson's Bay Company. James Douglas takes command.

1852 Site laid out; Fort Victoria becomes "Victoria."

1858 25,000 miners pass through Victoria on their way to Fraser River Gold Rush.

1862 Victoria incorporates as a city.

1866 Colonies of BC and Vancouver Island united. Capital moved to New Westminster on mainland.

1868 Victoria regains status as capital of BC.

1871 BC becomes province of Canada.

1880 Telephone lines installed between Victoria and Esquimalt Naval Base, west of the harbor.

1882 Hudson's Bay Co. gives Beacon Hill Park to Victoria.

1898 The Provincial Legislature buildings are completed.

1903 Ferry service begins between Sidney and Fraser River, linked to rails between Sidney and Victoria.

1905 The Canadian Pacific Railway begins construction of the Empress Hotel.

1914 World War I. Victoria International Airport, then named the Patricia Bay Airport, is constructed as a training site for the allied forces.

1945 The painter and writer Emily Carr dies.

1961 BC government establishes BC Ferry authority.

1994 Victoria hosts the XV Commonwealth Games.

Vancouver Island and Victoria

Vancouver Island, the largest island off North America's West Coast, is just 64 km (40 miles) from the mainland, separated from Vancouver by the Strait of Georgia to the east and from Washington State by the Strait of Juan de Fuca to the south and southeast. The island is 515 km (320 miles) long, with a population of approximately 689,000, nearly half of whom live in the Greater Victoria area.

Like the mainland, **Vancouver Island** was home to First Nations peoples for thousands of years and came under British rule, via the Hudson's Bay Company, with the building of **Fort Victoria** on the southern tip of the island in 1843. Five years later, Britain leased the island to Hudson's Bay with the stipulation that the company establish English colonies there. A few hundred pioneering souls did settle on farms around Victoria, but it was the 1858 Gold Rush that propelled the town from a backwater into what would eventually become the bustling capital of the new province of British Columbia.

Getting There

You can get to Victoria from Vancouver by ferry, airplane, seaplane, and helicopter. The fastest (and most expensive) way to go is by air. Harbour Air seaplanes (Tel. 250/385-2203 in Victoria; 604/688-1277 in Vancouver) and Helijet Airways (Tel. 250/382-6222 in Victoria; 604/273-1414 in Vancouver; toll free 800/665-4354) both offer 30-minute one-way flights daily. Air Canada and Canadian Airlines also have regularly scheduled service between Vancouver International and Victoria International airports. Otherwise, it's BC Ferry for the 1½-hour cruise between the ferry terminal at Tsawwassen and Swartz Bay. Daytrippers must keep

The BC ferry is a reliable way for you and your car to reach Victoria from Vancouver.

in mind that drive time from downtown Vancouver to Tsawwassen and from Swartz Bay to Victoria will add another 1½ hours one-way, making a driving trip to Vancouver Island a rather long day. Of course visitors do it all the time: by bus, on escorted tours, or in their own cars. If you just want to hit the surface of Victoria with a stop at the **Butchart Gardens**, check with Pacific Coach Lines (Tel. 800-661-1725, toll free) or one of the many other charter bus companies making this run.

Victoria

The capital of British Columbia is a 30-minute drive from the ferry terminal at Swartz Bay through bucolic country. However, it is bucolic only until you reach Victoria's suburbs, a thick, confusing development of housing, shopping malls, and fast-food restaurants. But carry on through the suburbs to the charming city itself. Highway 17 ends in the downtown business district right by the inner harbor.

Victoria, once a modest and quaint village beloved for its "veddy British" pretensions, now suffers a bit from its own overwhelming popularity. Old town streets are still flower-bedecked, but they are also stuffed with innumerable shops catering to summertime crowds, which will either make you quiver with anticipation or recoil in horror. Even the imperious **Empress Hotel** has seen fit to change with the times. Built by the Canadian Pacific Railway in 1908, this venerable hotel went and expanded her territory, adding a conference center in 1987 as part of a massive remodel. Modernization aside, taking tea at the Empress has always been considered an entirely valid reason to make a trip to Victoria. If you are determined to engage in that pursuit, be prepared for lines, exorbitant prices and for the less-than-unhurried experience of the tour-bus route.

A walk along the inner harbor and over the blue Johnson Street Bridge is a fine way to begin a tour of the city. Many of Victoria's famous Heritage buildings can be viewed here, including the Empress and the distinguished 1898 **Parliament Buildings**, all designed by Francis Rattenbury. (The **Visitors Information Centre** is also located just north of the bridge on the waterfront at 812 Wharf Street; Tel. 250/953-2033.) A delightful alternative to a bus tour at this point would be the 45-minute harbor tour on the **Victoria Harbour Ferry**. Passengers are entitled to disembark (and climb back aboard) at any of the ten stops along the way, including Chinatown and the **Point Ellice House** (2616 Pleasant Street; Tel. 250/380-6506), where you'll have another opportunity for afternoon tea (summers only from Thursday through Sunday) in the gardens of this lovely Victorian Heritage house.

Two-hour guided walking tours of the Inner Harbour or Old Town are available through the **Architectural Institute of British Columbia**. The free tours are given early each Tuesday through Saturday afternoon in July and August from the Blue Carrot Café in Bastion Square, but you must reserve a space by calling the Vancouver office

Tea at the venerable Empress Hotel is in itself worth the journey to beautiful Victoria, BC.

at (604) 683-8588, or toll-free (in BC only) at 800-667-0753, ext. 333.

On your own, you can gambol down **Government Street**, which links up with every point of interest in the small downtown Heritage District. Some of the stores worth a second look include Munro's, a much admired bookstore, and Rogers' Chocolates, because a little chocolate is a great incentive for recalcitrant (young) sightseers.

The **Royal British Columbia Museum** on the corner of Belleville and Government streets (open daily 9am-5pm; Tel. 250/356-7226) features high-impact experiential exhibits on the prehistory, history and natural history of BC and regional First Nations people. A National Geographic IMAX Theatre connected to the museum offers spectacular shows on nature up close and personal. The **Royal London Wax Museum** (two blocks west on Belleville Street) reveals what famous and infamous celebrities along with some lesser-known politicians wear when waxing poetic. Another Rattenbury-designed building, the **Crystal Garden**, sits on the corner of Belleville and Douglas streets; it is filled with tropical birds, plants, and gift-buying opportunities.

Continue down Government Street to Fort Street for a look around **Bastion Square**, the site of the original Fort Victoria and of the **Maritime Museum** (28 Bastion Square; Tel. 250/385-4222), which covers years of seafaring history. More restored 19th-century buildings are scattered along Yates Street, including the 1877 Deluge Fire Company Hall at 636 Yates. Victoria's **Chinatown**, Canada's oldest such enclave, is just another few blocks away on Fisgard Street. Fan Tan Alley, once the site of opium dens and gambling parlors, no longer has the sheen of naughtiness about it, but use your imagination.

Horse-drawn carriages line Menzies Street alongside the Legislative Buildings, waiting to clip-clop customers through a neighborhood of restored Victorian homes, including that of eccentric artist/author **Emily Carr** (1871-1945) at 207 Government Street. You can easily walk here, continuing south on Douglas Street to **Beacon Hill Park**. Flanked by Dallas Street and expansive views of the ocean, this 74-hectare (183-acre) green oasis dates from 1852, when it was declared a recreational reserve by James Douglas.

The Scandalous Mr. Rattenbury

Francis Mawson Rattenbury, who designed many of Victoria's most famous structures, including the Parliament Buildings, the Empress Hotel, and the Crystal Palace, was as much a victim of Victorian mores as he was a proponent —at least architecturally. Rattenbury arrived in Victoria from England in 1892 at the age of 25. The young and brash architect's reputation was soon made when he won the competition to design the city's Parliament Buildings. "Ratz," as he was nicknamed, went on to conceive private and public buildings throughout the province.

Whether success went to his head, or he succumbed to a midlife crisis, the second half of his life didn't go as smoothly as the first. In his mid-50s, the much celebrated Rattenbury left his wife for a younger woman, the multi-married, cigarette-smoking, and lovely Alma Packenham. Naturally, Victoria society snubbed the couple, and so they moved back to England, where Alma took up with their 17-year old chauffeur, George Stoner. In 1935, fearing that Rattenbury knew of their affair, Stoner clubbed the 68-year-old architect to death as he slept in an armchair. Alma committed suicide days after she was acquitted of murder, and Stoner, who had been sentenced to hang, was eventually released from prison.

*The 1898 Parliament Building—one of the distinguished
Heritage buildings designed by Francis Rattenbury.*

Glorious Gardens

The **Butchart Gardens**, located 21 km (13 miles) north of
Victoria off Highway 17 on the Saanich Inlet, are another
reason (along with tea at the Empress) that folks have been
flocking to Victoria for generations. Robert Butchart
arrived at Tod Inlet in 1902 and started a branch of the family's cement business in 1904. His wife, Jennie, took to
estate gardening with vigor, planting flowers and shrubs
around their home. As the gardens expanded, so did their
reputation. By 1930 Jennie Butchart had hosted thousands
of visitors, and today nearly one million people each year
flock to the grounds. Still family-owned, the site includes a
sunken garden planted in a former limestone quarry, a
Japanese garden with some stunning red maples and old
copper beech trees, and a concert lawn where summer
musical events and Saturday evening fireworks shows take

place. The summer season attracts many tour buses, and the wait for a table in the restaurants here can be lengthy. Happily, no matter what time of the year you find them, the Butchart Gardens will live up to expectations. (800 Benvenuto Ave., Brentwood Bay; Tel. 250/652-4422; toll-free: 866/652-4422)

On the way to Butchart Gardens, you'll pass a low-slung concrete building on the corner. This is **Butterfly Gardens**, a plant-filled resort for *Lepidoptera* of all sizes and shapes. Anyone (especially children) who loves these creatures will enjoy a walk through the humid greenhouse. (1461 Benvenuto Avenue; Tel. 250/652-3822; toll-free: 877/722-0272)

Sooke

If you have a car and time to explore, Highway 14, the West Coast Road, will take you to **Sooke**, a small fishing village 45 km (28 miles) from Victoria. Sooke is close enough to visit for a day, but worth an overnight stay if time permits. The **Sooke Harbour House** (see pages 133 and 141) is one of many inns in the area, and gourmands will want to make a pilgrimage to its restaurant for dinner. It's rated among the top dining spots in all of Canada.

The highway signs indicating Sooke "potholes" don't refer to car-rattling pits in the pavement. Instead, these pot-holes are natural rock pools in the Sooke River, which is a popular spot for bathing and picnicking. Hikers will have a field day in **East Sooke Regional Park**, where trails lead to beaches and an abandoned copper mine; for a challenging day hike, try the 10-km (6-mile) East Sooke Coast Trail. Stop at the **Sooke Museum/Information Centre** on Phillips Road (off Highway 14) for directions to this and other parks and beaches.

WHAT TO DO

W hether you lean toward physical activity, artistic pur-
suits, shopping, or late-night club hopping,
Vancouver is well equipped to meet your needs. While the
city might not be considered a mecca of cultural sophistication when compared to, say, New York or London, there's
always something happening and somewhere stimulating to
go. Given its status as one of the most livable and attractive
cities in the world, Vancouver is a regular stop for touring
musicians and theatrical shows. But what makes it a lively
place day and night are the sheer numbers of residents eager
to make the most of their after-work hours.

ENTERTAINMENT AND NIGHTLIFE

The weekly *Georgia Straight* newspaper is your best source
for entertainment listings if you want to investigate the thriving club and lounge scene around the city. For the ever-
growing number of venues that require preplanning (for
example, theaters, concert halls, and top jazz clubs), find out
what's scheduled during your stay by calling Vancouver's
24-hour Arts Hotline (Tel. 604/684-2787) or check their web
site on the Internet at http://www.allianceforarts.com.

Classical Music and Opera

You'll find many outlets for classical music in the city. The
Vancouver Symphony Orchestra plays at the glorious
Orpheum Theatre (Granville Street at Smithe Street; Tel.
604/876-3434), which opened in 1927, and in various out-
door venues during the summer. The Vancouver Recital
Society brings a mix of talented musicians to the Vancouver
Playhouse (Hamilton Street at Dunsmuir Street; Tel.
604/602-0363), and you'll want to find out who's perform-

Summer is time for Shakespeare-in-the-tents at the annual Bard-on-the-Beach festival in Vanier Park.

ing at the acoustically and architecturally brilliant Chan Centre for the Performing Arts at UBC (6265 Crescent Road; Tel. 604/822-2697). The Vancouver Opera Association produces five full-length operas each season at the Queen Elizabeth Theatre. For ticket information, call (604) 465-3050.

Theater and Pop Concerts

Live theater runs the gamut from professional Broadway road companies to locally bred groups performing chestnuts of world drama. Big touring companies tend to come to the Queen Elizabeth Theatre (Hamilton and Dunsmuir Streets), while you'll find a wide range of concerts—dance, comedy, jazz, blues, pop, and more exotic groups—at the adjoining Vancouver Playhouse as well as at the Orpheum (Smithe and Seymour). Tel. for all three: (604) 665-3050. The Arts Club

Theatre on Granville Island is a slightly more casual place to see revivals of classic plays. After years of planning and a $9 million renovation, the Arts Club opened its newest space, the 650-seat Stanley Theatre (2750 Granville Street; Tel. 604/687-1644). Catch musicals, revues, and dramas featuring Canadian writers and artists in this former movie palace.

Summer visitors have another two stages to enjoy; both are outdoors. For Shakespeare lovers, borrow a pillow and hie thee to Vanier Park for "Bard-on-the-Beach" (Tel. 604/739-0559), where three plays are performed in repertory throughout the summer inside tents with the loveliest backdrop imaginable—English Bay. Over in Stanley Park, local actors mingle with semi-professionals under the banner of "Theatre Under The Stars" (Malkin Bowl, Tel. 604/687-0174), where performances of old Broadway favorites are given in July and August. Those in the know recommend umbrellas, mosquito repellent, and a cushion to sit on. If you crave the less conventional, such as new theater, performance art, jazz, exotic dance, or comedy, the Vancouver East Cultural Centre, known as "The Cultch" (1895 Venables Street; Tel. 604/251-1363), is the place to be—an intimate hall with an eclectic crowd. Housed in a former church, programs include children's theater and chamber music. Also check out the Firehall Arts Centre (280 East Cordova Street; Tel. 604/689-0926) for provocative, innovative performances.

Dance

Contemporary and classical dance fans who visit outside the summer months have the opportunity to see a variety of dance companies at the Queen Elizabeth Theatre or at the Firehall Arts Centre. In July, look for the two-week "Dancing on the Edge" Festival, with cutting-edge choreography performed on street corners and on more traditional stages. Call the Arts Hotline (604/684-2787) for schedules and ticket information.

Film

Movies are big business here both on screen and around town, since Vancouver has become the third most popular city for filmmaking after Los Angeles and New York City. Granville Street between Georgia and Smithe streets supports a number of multi-screen, first-run movie complexes. For international and "art" films, the Pacific Cinematheque (1131 Howe Street; Tel. 604/688-3456) is the local cinemaphile's choice. If you've never experienced one of those larger-than-life, big-sound, wraparound, special-format screens that end in "-max," there are two in Vancouver: an Omnimax Theatre at Science World (see page 47) and an IMAX Theatre at Canada Place (see page 34). A visit to either makes a good outing on a wet day.

Clubs

As evidenced by the throngs of young people lining up to get into some of the more popular night spots, Vancouverites (and energetic 19-year-olds from the States who can legally drink here) just love a party. You may want to assess the patrons waiting patiently in the rope line before paying any cover charges, especially if kids in disco wear make you giggle. Again, the *Georgia Straight* gives fairly accurate descriptions of the clubs, but different nights attract different crowds.

Blues fans will appreciate The Yale (1300 Granville Street; Tel. 604/681-9253), a funky, brick-walled bar with a dance floor and a reliable lineup of local and traveling musicians. The Fairview Pub (898 West Broadway; Tel. 604/872-1262) is another casual club that features good lively blues bands and dancing, and a no-smoking policy, except for an isolated cubicle. The Arts Club Theatre's Backstage Lounge on Granville Island also regularly schedules blues musicians, in an atmosphere that is comparatively upscale.

Vancouver Goes to the Movies

If you notice a group of large white trailers hogging all the parking spaces on city streets, it means a movie or television show is being filmed nearby. The motion picture industry began a flirtation with British Columbia in the 1920s, shooting *The Alaskan* in 1924 and footage for *Rosemarie* in 1936, among others. But despite the area's varied and gorgeous scenery, stardom eluded the province until the late 1970s.

Producers began taking the region seriously when they discovered the low Canadian dollar had a positive effect on production costs. British Columbia, sensing the beginnings of a beautiful relationship, hustled to provide facilities and crews. Filmmaking now accounts for over a half-billion dollars for the local economy and employment for approximately 25,000 British Columbians.

A few of the movies filmed in BC include *Five Easy Pieces*, *McCabe and Mrs. Miller*, *Carnal Knowledge*, *Little Women*, *The Scarlet Letter*, *Jumanji*, *Legends of the Fall*, *This Boy's Life*, and *The Accused*. TV's "The X-Files" was shot in Vancouver until recently, and television shows currently produced in and around the city include "Outer Limits," "So Weird," "The New Addams Family," and "Millennium."

Hoping to see those trailers? The BC Film Commission regularly publishes a list of projects currently in production, which can be had for the taking at the BC Business Information Centre, The Station, 601 West Cordova. The commission also operates a film hotline; call (604) 660-3569.

Outdoor music is one of the many summer perks enjoyed by Vancouverites and visitors.

You'll find more adults at these lounges than at some of the other well-advertised clubs such as Richard's on Richards (1036 Richards Street; Tel. 604/687-6794), where a huge space features revolving mirror balls, bulky bouncers, and pulsating music—a bit over the top unless you're 20, in which case you might think it's cool. And speaking of "cool," Bar-None in Yaletown (1222 Hamilton Street; Tel. 604/689-7000) and BaBalu at the Comfort Inn Downtown (formely the Hotel Dakota) (see page 127) are two of the current trendy spots for drinking and cigar smoking. Pool players can try for a table at the Yaletown Pub (see page 137). For a sedate evening, try the Gerard Lounge at the Sutton Place Hotel (see page 130) or the Wedgewood Hotel Lounge (see page 130). Both have pianists playing standards, and you won't feel out of place in a suit or a cocktail dress.

SHOPPING

The shopping's great in Vancouver, but don't expect to stock up on bargains unless you have a favorable exchange rate or you happen to be in town after Boxing Day, when the winter sales begin. For souvenirs, don't overlook museum gift shops, which often have a much more varied selection of knickknacks than the tourist-oriented stores.

What to Buy and Where to Buy It

Books

Per capita, British Columbians read more than any other group of Canadians, and you'll find well-stocked bookstores downtown and in every neighborhood. BC's largest is the University of BC Bookstore at 6200 University Boulevard. Cookbook aficionados should definitely look into Barbara-Jo's Books to Cooks in at 1128 Mainland Street in Yaletown. The new age bookstore Banyan Books at 2671 W Broadway is a good place for meeting like-minded people.

Clothing

There is a plethora of upscale men's clothiers in the Pacific Centre Mall (West Georgia Street at Hornby), due to its proximity to the financial center of the city. There's also an

Sinclair Centre is one of a number of Vancouver malls where well-heeled men can update their wardrobes.

entrance in this mall to Holt Renfrew, a small department store with an expensive but prime stock of apparel and shoes for men and women. After surveying the shopping areas here, on Robson Street or in any major mall, you might decide most shops resemble each other. However, one small chain is worth mentioning, as it sells clothes designed and manufactured locally. Called A-Wear, their store in the Sinclair Centre (see page 35) is handsome and staffed with helpful salespeople. And over on the East Side, tucked into Commercial Drive's mix of produce stands, delicatessens, and funky shops, lies one terrific Italian shoe store.

Gifts, Food, and Furnishings

Robson Street has long been considered the place for visitors to shop, and while it holds a wide variety of shops and many recognizable labels, there is also a strong element of "tourist trapism" along the way. Still, you'll want to walk its length from Burrard to Denman just for the experience and to gape at the crowds. Do stop in at the Lush outlet, which is one in a local chain of soap shops and a very enticing place to stock up on delicious-smelling natural balms and bath items. There are a number of places selling smoked salmon, but sample the goods first before shipping any off as gifts from the Pacific Northwest. For a taste of old Vancouver (by way of Scotland), try Murchies at 970 Robson for coffee and tea and the supplies to brew them (one of nine Murchies outlets).

In the 1980s the warehouses of Yaletown became trendy restaurants, boutiques, cafés and artists' residences. The shopping there leans toward home décor and clothing stores. Another enjoyable street for browsing is West 4th in Kitsilano between Burrard and Alma streets. Because it's essentially the neighborhood shopping district, you'll find everything from the local natural foods grocery to kitchen gear and sporting goods.

Granville Island is as popular with the locals as it is with visitors, which makes it quite busy—especially on the weekends, when it's best to arrive via public transportation to avoid the parking hassles. The Public Market here carries all manner of fresh produce, flowers, fish, meat, and really anything else one could desire in the way of food. There's also an excellent coffee bar, plus stalls selling bread, chocolate, and pastries. It's the place to browse for breakfast or to create a picnic lunch. In adjacent converted warehouses, you'll find crafts, blown glass, textiles, and other handmade works of art displayed and sold in small galleries; many of the artists here maintain studios on the island. If you have children in tow, be prepared to settle in for a few hours in the Kids Only department store across from the Granville Island Brewery. The second floor features an arcade in which players collect tickets for points scored in the games. The tickets may then be redeemed for trinkets at a nearby counter, an exercise that can take a long time for indecisive little ones.

South Granville from 16th Avenue to the bridge is a good street for antiques, designer goods, and high-end gifts. Just park the car or get off the bus and walk up and down until it's time for a coffee. You won't have far to go to find a peaceful sidewalk café.

Gastown is the prime consumer location for T-shirts, Maple Leaf key chains, and other "Guess Who Visited Vancouver?" items. However, there are also two government-licensed galleries here that specialize in Northwest Coast and Inuit arts and crafts: the Inuit Gallery of Vancouver (206 Cambie Street) and Images for A Canadian Heritage (164 Water Street).

SPORTS

It's exhausting just thinking about the array of sporting activities one can indulge in around a city that never stays indoors for too long. In brief, if the sport's been invented, you can probably find somewhere to try it in Vancouver.

On Land

Hiking and Walking

Within the city limits, Stanley Park has easy forest trails and the 10-km (6-mile) seawall path should be part of every itinerary. You can also walk in Pacific Spirit Park (see page 51) on the UBC campus. For a leisurely stroll, there's the 5-km (3-mile) path through Vanier Park to Kitsilano Beach.

Outside the city, you have mountains and forests to choose from. Lighthouse Park in West Vancouver ends at an old lighthouse with stunning views of the city after a 10-minute walk through virgin temperate rainforest. And you needn't return to the car once you reach Point Atkinson: there are additional trails to explore here with equally exceptional vistas. There's a strenuous hike up Grouse Mountain (often closed due to storm damage, see page 60), or you can take the chairlift to the Black Mountain trails in Cypress Provincial Park farther west. For other day hikes, try Lynn Canyon Park (see page 57) or Lower Seymour Conservation Reserve (see page 59).

> **Heed signs to walk your bike on parts of the exercise paths in Stanley Park; they signal heavier pedestrian use.**

Cycling

You can easily rent bicycles and helmets (required by law) on Denman or Georgia streets near Stanley Park and spend

At Blackcomb Resort youngsters practice their climbing skills for the authentic rock faces that can't be far away.

a day biking around the city. The River Road bike path in Steveston, which can be reached on the west side of the Dunsmuir Bridge, is lengthy and flat and makes an easy ride for kids. (See page 107 for general guidelines on cycling in Vancouver.)

Golf

Within the city limits, the University Golf Club is open to the public (5185 University Boulevard; Tel. 604/224-1818). Otherwise, try the Furry Creek Golf and Country Club near Horseshoe Bay or the lovely new courses in Whistler and Pemberton.

Skiing

The inveterate skier already knows about Whistler and Blackcomb Mountains in what the travel magazines describe as the finest ski area in North America (see page 65). Even Britain's Prince William is a fan of these slopes. But for the day skier or for anyone who just wants to play a bit in the snow, Grouse Mountain and Cypress Bowl on the North Shore provide a quick fix. Each also operates a ski school.

On the Water

Kayaking

It's not difficult to learn the basics of sea kayaking quickly. Novices to the sport can take a lesson at the Ecomarine Ocean Kayak Centre on Granville Island (Tel. 604/689-7575) or on Bowen Island at Bowen Island Sea Kayaking (Tel. 1-800-60-Kayak or 604/947-9266; also bike rentals and tours). Then it's off to paddle around in the bay or Howe Sound, either escorted or on your own.

Swimming

The beaches from English Bay to Spanish Banks offer fine saltwater swimming; lifeguards are on duty during the summer months. Kitsilano Beach pool is open from May to September and the pool at Second Beach is open in the summer. All year long, the facilities at the Vancouver Aquatic Centre in the West End, which include an Olympic-sized indoor pool, are open to the public.

Fishing and Sailing

Many whale-watching charter boat companies are located in Victoria. One is Ocean Explorations (www.oceanexplorations.com; Tel. 250/383-6722). For yacht cruises and sport fishing, check into the charter boats at Coal Harbour behind the Westin Bayshore.

Spectator Sports

Baseball

Vancouver is home to the Triple-A Vancouver Canadians baseball team. During the season (April to October), games are played in the charming 7,000-seat Nat Bailey Stadium, across the street from Queen Elizabeth Park. Tickets may be purchased at the stadium on game days, but you should call first to check availability (Tel. 604/872-5232).

Football

BC Place is the venue to catch the BC Lions football team from June through October. For information, call (604) 589-7627; tickets may be purchased through Ticketmaster at (604) 280-4400.

Hockey

The Vancouver Canucks usually make the play-offs in the National Hockey League, and are the most popular sports team in Vancouver. If you can score tickets to a home game at the relatively new GM Place Stadium, it's sure to be exciting. The regular season lasts from September through April (Tel. 604/899-4625).

VANCOUVER FOR CHILDREN

On the windows of various Vancouver attractions, you might notice stickers indicating that the premises are especially suitable for children, as designated by the group "Kid Friendly Vancouver." In fact, the entire city pretty much qualifies for this description. Vancouver is a children's paradise, with plenty of outdoor activities and relatively few "educational" opportunities to ruin an otherwise good time.

In addition, the transportation possibilities via AquaBus, SeaBus, SkyTrain, and ferry all add to the excitement of discovering a new city.

If the weather's good, any of the beaches from English Bay to Spanish Banks beg to be explored. In particular, Second Beach in Stanley Park has a playground for small children and a wonderful pool with water slides. Of course, Stanley Park in its entirety is a kid magnet. The Vancouver

Vancouver's Children's Festival

One annual event underscores Vancouver's fondness for its youngest residents: the Vancouver International Children's Festival, now over 20 years old. For a solid week beginning the last Monday in May, two dozen red-and-white striped tents take over Vanier Park. They cover the stages that present theater, music, dance, storytelling, and puppetry shows by children's performers from across Canada and around the world.

Enhancing the performances are local talent (children's choruses and dance groups), food booths, and a marketplace selling books, musical instruments, and T-shirts. Festival sponsors underwrite special workshop tents where attendees can make kites, create art and costumes from recycled materials, play music, or get their hands on some 40,000 Legos.

Vancouver's festival is the prototype on which similar celebrations for children have been modeled all over the world. Like the city that inspired it, it continues to evolve, most recently introducing the "X-Site," with theater, visual arts, and literary arts programming for teenagers. For information or the festival brochure, contact the organizers at (604) 708-5655 or check out their website at www.vancouverchildrensfestival.com. Tickets can be purchased through Ticketmaster (Tel. 604/280-4444, or online at www.ticketmaster.ca).

Aquarium (see page 33), with colorful fish, strange insects, and regularly scheduled Beluga whale shows, is a must-stop with kids, and even a walk on the old logging trails should hold their interest. Feeding the voracious and cheeky black squirrels that overrun the forest is not advised, by the way.

Kids will be under the impression that Granville Island is their personal amusement park, between the Kids Only store, the entertaining buskers, and the nearby adventure and water playground. Vanier Park is another haven where you can spend the better part of a day. The Vancouver Museum and the Pacific Space Centre share a building here (don't miss the humorous planetarium shows), and the Maritime Museum includes a hands-on maritime play area. When it's time to get some fresh air, head toward the shore and walk to Kitsilano Beach. A visit to the Museum of Anthropology at UBC may qualify as one of those dreaded learning experiences, but most school-aged kids will be won over by the canoes, photographs, and beautiful Native American carvings.

The Van Dusen Botanical Gardens is another worthy stop as a walk through the Elizabethan hedge maze (one of only three in North America) will provoke many giggles. If you're seeking something to do indoors, Science World provides plenty of hands-on experiments and live science shows with an emphasis for younger kids. St. Andrew's-Wesley Church (Burrard and Nelson streets) presents Jazz Vespers, free, Sundays at 4 pm (Tel. 604/683-4574) but most young ones would rather be surfing indoors at the Newton Wave Pool, 13730–72 Ave Surrey. Tel. 604/501-5540.

> Every spring the parks board cleans up the beaches and places rows of logs on the sand for people to sit on.

In North Vancouver, a ride up Grouse Mountain in the gondola will be memorable, and there's plenty to do once you arrive at the top all year 'round, including jumping on the chair lift to get to the next peak. (Skip the food at the patio near the Skyride exit and head up the hill to the outdoor grill near the lift instead.) Tired parents needing rest might convince the kids to visit two orphaned grizzly bear cubs at the new Wildlife Refuge followed by a Northwest Indian style dinner with traditional dancing at Hiwus Feasthouse (Tel. 604/980-9311). On the way to Grouse, stop at the Capilano Fish Hatchery in Capilano Park to observe the growth of salmon from fry to adults heading for spawning grounds. Or thrill the kids with a walk over the Capilano Suspension Bridge. The management at this tourist stop gives kids a "passport" at the entrance, which can be stamped at different points in the park and redeemed for a certificate in the gift shop. It's an effective way to keep the kids moving.

Outdoor exercise is easy to find in and around Vancouver, whether it's on land or in the water.

Further afield, a ferry ride to Bowen Island is only 20 minutes from Horseshoe Bay, and the destination is itself out of the ordinary. Two-person kayaks can be rented on the dock (see page 63) and kids will thrill to be on the water. Just insist they help paddle.

Festivals and Special Events

Vancouver celebrates the arts with major international festivals. Summer is particularly active, so make reservations in advance. Call (604) 683-2000 to request printed information, including a complete listing of events and dates; or visit www.guestlife.com/vancouver/events.

January–February: Chinese New Year Festival; Women in View Festival

March: Vancouver Storytelling Festival

April: Vancouver Playhouse International Wine Festival

May: Vancouver International Children's Festival; New Music West international music festival

June: Du Maurier International Jazz Festival; Alcan Dragon Boat Festival; Bard on the Beach

July: The 10-day Dancing on the Edge Festival; Vancouver Folk Music Festival; Chamber Music Festival; Symphony of Fire (fireworks)

August: Out on Screen (gay and lesbian film festival); Pacific National Exhibition; Vancouver International Comedy Festival; Fringe Festival (theater, comedy, dance, music, improv, etc.)

September: Molson Indy Vancouver

October: Vancouver International Film Festival; Vancouver International Writers and Readers Festival

December: Christmas Carol Ship Parade

EATING OUT

Vancouverites are known to be pretty modest about their city and its attributes, so most would probably hesitate to apply superlatives to Vancouver's restaurants. Given the relatively recent emergence of Vancouver as a destination, how could its food possibly rank with that of such culinary centers as San Francisco, Chicago, and New York?

Those in the know might forcefully counter that Vancouver is already a player on the world food scene. But everyone would agree that there have been momentous, welcome changes in the restaurant industry. It wasn't so long ago that dining out in Vancouver meant Chinese or Italian or Greek food from menus that hadn't veered off course from the day the restaurants opened. Special-occasion meals called for reservations at the steak house. While some of those establishments are still thriving, the idea of what it means to eat out has taken a sea change in the minds of many. An evening out to dinner is now as much about having an experience—the food, the wine, the atmosphere—as it is about filling one's stomach. Perhaps more so. And an ever-growing number of chefs are guiding the way with innovative, seasonal, and artistic dishes that reflect a great passion for food and presentation.

That's not to say dining out in Vancouver has become stuffy or pretentious. Vancouver is happy with its reputation as a laid-back city where "smart-casual" is about as dressy as one need get. The staff in the majority of restaurants, no matter how renowned the reputation, are refreshingly free of attitude. And the diners themselves demand value. Vancouverites aren't particularly anxious to throw their dollars about, but they do like to eat out as often as possible. Since restaurants must rely on a local following to get them through the long winters, it's becoming increasingly easier to get a great meal at a reasonable price.

Vancouver's ambiance also drives the food scene. The health-conscious locals prefer light, flavorful dishes, and chefs are a step ahead, substituting essences of stocks and broths for heavy sauces and making a huge demand on Fraser Valley farmers for innovative greens and organic fruits and produce throughout the year. The province's bounty of seafood provides the basis for everything from a simple salmon steak, to grilled scallops wrapped in

High tea in the Fairmont Hotel lounge is one way to dine in style in Vancouver.

octopus bacon, to raw shellfish bars that bring tears to otherwise toughened oyster zealots. Vancouver's multiculturalism also played a major role in the revolution. Pacific Northwest meets Pacific Rim and fusion marries ingredients that don't necessarily speak the same language but know how to have a good time on Italian-pottery plates.

When and Where to Eat

In general, Vancouver hotels do not include breakfast in the price of a room; however, a few provide a continental breakfast. But you'll find plenty of cafés, coffee shops, and bakeries where you can get a bite to tide you over until lunch. Some eateries serve breakfast all day, or at least until 2 or

3pm. Fancy "brunch" is always available at the big hotels, but you can also create your own late-morning meal while shopping at such emporia as the Granville Public Market. Sampling the fare while strolling through the city's shopping districts is the best way to discover what Vancouverites eat for lunch, and your choices here are as varied as the city's neighborhoods.

When it comes to the evening meal, this isn't Barcelona. The locals are buttering their bread by 7 or 8pm and kitchens begin closing at 10pm, although you'll find a few open until 11. Once you decide what time you'll be ready for dinner, the more difficult question to answer is where to eat.

Fine Dining

If you're interested in sampling the best of what Vancouver offers in fine dining, your choices are vast. While locals don't usually scamper to eat at hotel restaurants, many of these kitchens are turning out outstanding dishes. In particular, Diva at the Met has been getting lots of attention from the "Best of" lists, but there are many others with exceptional food and service. Of the many locally owned white-table-cloth eateries, Bishop's is always on the tip of every gourmet's tongue. Many chefs received their start in the kitchen of this West 4th Street institution, and John Bishop can be personally credited with spicing up the city's culinary stew. For unbiased advice on restaurants outside the listings in the back of this book, turn to *City Foods* or the weekly *Georgia Straight*, free publications you'll find in bookstores and cafés.

Handsome neighborhood restaurants are cropping up, offering comforting menus at affordable prices to keep the regulars happy and the tourists elated. This welcome trend is best exemplified by intimate spaces such as Étoile, on

Wild About Salmon

Salmon is the reigning king of the waters in British Columbia, first revered by Coast Salish Natives who survived on the abundant fish. Salmon was even the province's major export for a short period of time in the 1800s, prior to the completion of the railway. The Fraser River still provides two-thirds of the area's total sockeye catch, but other salmon, particularly coho, have suffered from over-fishing and habitat destruction.

There are five different types of salmon. Chinook (or king) salmon is the largest of them all, with firm ivory to deep-red flesh. Commercial harvests are small. Chum salmon flesh ranges from pale to medium red and is often canned under the name of keta salmon. Coho salmon, a popular, moderately priced variety is no longer readily available due to its status as a threatened species. Sockeye salmon is the mainstay of the commercial fishing industry, with a firm, deep-red flesh. Pink salmon is the smallest of the lot and is usually canned.

Restaurants in BC seldom omit salmon, either wild or farmed, local or imported, from the menu. Fresh wild salmon is available seasonally from June through September. Farmed salmon, much of which comes from the waters off Vancouver Island, is available year 'round. Is there a difference in taste between wild and farmed? According to some gourmands, there is. But given the opportunity, you can decide for yourself which is preferable.

To see and learn more about these ancient creatures, head to Capilano Regional Park in North Vancouver and walk to the fish hatchery (4500 Capilano Park Road; Tel. 604/666-1790). Breeding tanks, a glass-fronted observation deck, and displays combine to show and tell the fascinating life-cycle of the salmon.

Hornby Street. It won't take a great deal of trouble to find the gems, so ask around for recommendations, make reservations, and don't settle for what's convenient or for any place where the food is secondary to a theme or a T-shirt. Even if you come from a place where great meals are commonplace, Vancouver chefs will delight your palate.

Ethnic Vancouver

Multiculturalism adds immeasurably to a city, especially when it comes time to eat. In Vancouver, it's a certainty that adventurous, curious, or merely gung-ho eaters won't be disappointed with the range of food available. You'll easily find French, Italian, Greek, and Chinese restaurants, but with a little investigation you can also discover Hungarian, Japanese, Indian, Korean, Southeast Asian, and even Mexican and Native American eateries. So if you need to redirect a debate on where to eat, decide instead what type of food you'd like to try. Excellent Chinese restaurants abound,

Sockeye it to 'em — Salmon is the undisputed heavyweight underwater champion in British Columbia.

with some of the finest located in the nearby suburb of Richmond. And for food from India (particularly if you've never tried any), Vij's is the last word.

Casual Dining

If you're satisfied with a Continental breakfast, you'll find fresh baked goods and coffee on practically every street corner. Otherwise, you can fill up for a long day of sightseeing at Sophie's Cosmic Cafe on West 4th Street. Along Robson Street and Denman Street there are many sidewalk cafés and casual restaurants serving lunch and dinner. The public market on Granville Island is another wonderful place to find breakfast, lunch, snacks, baked goods, and deli items. You'll always have better luck finding reasonably priced places to eat outside the downtown business district. Try Commercial Drive for pizza and Italian food, West Broadway for Greek fare, and West 4th Street for vegetarian choices.

> **You won't find much street food in Vancouver, but when you do, it's likely to be vegetarian "hot dogs."**

What and Where to Drink

The Word on Wine

Vancouverites are statistically the highest per-capita consumers of wine in any North American city. Many restaurants pride themselves on their cellars, featuring bottles from every wine-growing region in the world including the province's own Okanagan Valley. Wine is relatively expensive, however. Alcohol sales are strictly controlled (and highly taxed) by the British Columbia Liquor Distribution Branch (BCLDB), so purchasing wine, beer, or spirits outside of restaurants and bars isn't as straightforward as walking into a corner convenience store. There are a few private wine shops and some beer and wine outlets connected to pubs, but if you wish to buy liquor, you'll need to find a BCLDB store. Downtown, there's one at 1120 Alberni Street. Call the BCLDB wine line at (604) 660-9463 for hours and information. BCLDB stores do not accept credit cards. For wine only, try the private Marquis Wine Cellars downtown (1034 Davie Street) or the Broadway International Wine Shop (2752 West Broadway).

Beers and Breweries

Beer is not native to Vancouver, but based on its importance to the population, the suds rank right up there with sunny days and the Canucks hockey team. Two breweries, the Red Cross Brewing Company and the Vancouver Brewery, opened in Vancouver in 1882, four years before the city's incorporation. Through mergers and acquisitions, these original companies have since disappeared, but small breweries (or microbreweries) have spread throughout the province.

Due to complicated Canadian liquor laws, you can't purchase beer from the manufacturer unless it operates a brewpub: a special venue where beer is both made and imbibed. It's thus possible to tour a regular brewery, but to sample the wares you'll have to go elsewhere. One local brewery that offers tours is Granville Island Brewing Company (Tel. 604/687-2739). Some popular local brew-pubs include Yaletown Brewing at 1111 Mainland in Yaletown; Steamworks Brewing at 375 Water Street in Gastown; and, in North Vancouver, Sailor Hägar's BrewPub at 375 Semisch Avenue.

Crazy for Caffeine

Walking down Robson Street, you'll eventually be confronted with the vision of two Starbucks coffee shops holding down opposite corners. You aren't seeing double. This is

Coffee, tea, or cappuccino? Caffeine takes on many forms in many venues throughout Vancouver.

merely one indication that you've arrived in a town devoted to caffeine. Whether this is due to its proximity to Seattle (the home of Starbucks) or to the high number of rainy days isn't clear. But coffee reigns supreme and coffee bars can be found in bookstores, laundromats, office buildings, strip malls, and just about anywhere else there's an electrical outlet for the cappuccino maker.

Perplexed by the lingo? "A double half-and-half, lowfat, no-foam latte, please" is just the easy way to request two shots of espresso, one decaffeinated and one regular, with steamed 2% milk but without the foam on top. Tell the barista what you want and they will make it for you, with or without the fancy lingo. You may also notice jars or cans gracing the counters of coffeehouses that do not provide table service. If you feel the urge, drop your change in there as a tip.

HANDY TRAVEL TIPS

An A–Z Summary of Practical Information

(Note: all prices quoted in Canadian dollars unless otherwise indicated)

A

ACCOMMODATIONS

"Gassy" Jack Deighton, who opened the first saloon in Gastown in 1867, but the taxman soon appeared at his door telling him to operate a hotel or lose his liquor permit. He opened Deighton House in 1870, and although it was destroyed in the Great Fire of 1886 along with nearly every other building in town, the hospitality business already had a firm foothold in what soon became Vancouver. By the following year the first Hotel Vancouver had opened, and the city has seen a steady rise in room numbers ever since. Today, new hotels are currently under construction, while many older properties have recently been renovated or are in the process of having a facelift. Even when enjoying high occupancy rates, Vancouver hoteliers don't coast on their reputations.

Depending on your budget, options range from humble motor lodges to luxurious AAA five-diamond properties featuring knowledgeable concierges, courtesy limousine service, and health spas. While it can be rewarding to explore more "off-the-beaten-track" locations for lodging (such as the North Shore), the majority of rooms are located downtown, convenient to every part of the metropolitan area by public transportation, private car, or taxi. Downtown hotels tend to be fairly large (better for attracting convention business), although the industry is slowly jumping on the "boutique" hotel bandwagon.

There are a handful of small hotels downtown and a fair number of B&Bs in other neighborhoods for those who prefer more intimate digs. To obtain a registry of inns and bed-and-breakfasts, contact the British Columbia Bed and Breakfast Association at (604) 734-3486. For the truly budget-minded, the University of British Columbia rents student housing during the summer, with a few units available during the school year. Call (604) 822-1000 for information and reservations.

Vancouver

It is highly recommended to reserve rooms in advance, especially during the summer when you will be competing with the endless stream of cruise ships that port here on their way to Alaska. Rates are at their highest from April through October, with July and August commanding extra-top dollar, particularly in resorts on the outlying islands. Vancouver is a popular convention town so the big hotels can also book up during the least likely times. Vancouver Central Reservations will help tel. 1888 895-2870 or 604 904-7080; from the UK tel. 0880 731-6387. Hotel taxes add another 17 percent to your bill: 10 percent for the provincial hotel and motel room sales tax, and 7 percent for the GST, which is refundable if you send in your receipt and a refund form, available at your hotel (see MONEY MATTERS below). If you have a car, hotel parking costs from $7 to $18 a day.

AIRPORTS

Vancouver International Airport is located in the suburb of Richmond, about 20 minutes from downtown Vancouver. Expanded in 1996, it now sports a new international terminal that leads passengers in smooth succession through Canadian customs to the baggage claim area. (The original terminal is now the gateway to flights within Canada.) All the major rental car companies are steps away from the exit doors, making pick-up and drop-off easy and efficient. Taxis are readily available and cost approximately $21 to downtown sites; you'll pay a bit more during rush hour. The green Airporter bus ($10 one-way, $17 round trip) is also available outside the baggage claim area, but it stops at virtually every downtown hotel, creating an interminable ride if you happen to be staying somewhere near the end of the bus loop. Unless you are traveling solo and on a tight budget, don't inconvenience yourself.

An airport assessment fee is charged upon departure once you pass customs on your way home: $5 for domestic flights, $10 to the US, and $15 on other international flights. Credit cards are accepted. Also, if you haven't quite finished shopping, it's good to know that the airport shops charge the same prices that you'd pay in town.

B

BICYCLE RENTAL

Cycling around the Stanley Park seawall will make you think you're a local. The marked path continues past English Bay, and you can even take your wheels over to Granville Island on designated AquaBus routes. Inquire if your hotel has bikes to loan; otherwise, you can rent bicycles and/or roller blades along Denman Street at any of several shops between Georgia and Alberni. For complete information on bike paths, pick up a free *Cycling in Vancouver* map at bike shops, libraries, and community centers; on the Internet check out www.city.vancouver.bc.ca/engsvcs/transport/cycling/bikepage. In Steveston, there are 10 km (6 miles) of bike and walking paths along the dikes around Garry Point Park. Remember that helmets are required for bicyclists.

BUDGETING FOR YOUR TRIP

Vancouver isn't an inexpensive destination, even during the low season, but much also depends on where the Canadian dollar is relative to your country's currency. Travelers from the US have been enjoying highly favorable rates recently, transforming fancy $200 hotel rooms into US$130 bargains. When budgeting, decide how much you can afford to spend, divide it by the number of days you'll be on holiday, then plan your lodging and meal choices to accommodate your pocketbook (and add another 20 percent just in case). If you are flexible and can travel in late autumn or winter, you'll save on entrance fees at most attractions and get great deals at hotels.

Accommodations. Expect to pay from $75 for a small double at a plain hotel like the extremely popular Sylvia to $360 for an executive double at a posh hotel such as the Wedgewood. Remember to add another 17 percent for taxes and about $15 per day for parking.

Meals. Vancouverites are becoming sensitive to price when it comes to dining out, and many eateries are responding to the pressure to keep prices reasonable. In general, entrées at the better restaurants start at $16 à la carte and can easily reach $28 or more. Ethnic restaurants are usually quite a bit less expensive, as are restaurants outside the central business district. Portions are generous nearly everywhere you go.

Transportation. Buses arrive frequently on most street corners and cost $2.00 (exact change required) one-way in town, a little more to the outlying areas. Taxi fare from downtown to Kitsilano will run around $10. The short hop on the AquaBus from Hornby to Granville Island is $1.75. If you have a car, plan to pay for parking wherever you go: most pay lots take credit cards and charge $2–$6 per hour. Street parking requires change for the meters, except in residential districts. Ferries to Vancouver Island cost about $50 if you are taking a car, plus another $12 per person. Rental cars (see below) will add another $250 or more per week, not including gasoline.

Attractions. You'll be paying from $5 for entrance to the tiny Canadian Crafts Museum to about $25 per person to walk around Victoria's Butchart Gardens. If money is a factor, decide ahead of time where to disburse your sightseeing dollars.

C

CAMPING

Should you wish to camp in a provincial park or in Pacific Rim National Park Reserve, you'll need to make reservations. Go online at www.discovercamping.ca, or phone (604) 689-9025 (or toll-free in North America: 800-689-9025). For the West Coast Trail in PRNPR, call (250) 387-1642 or toll-free in N.A. 800-435-5622.

CAR RENTAL

Although public transportation is quite good (if crowded) and driving can be hectic in the city, a car will make your visit to any of the islands or out-of-downtown destinations more convenient. If you need a car for only part of your trip, you might want to hire one on an as-needed basis. It does pay to compare prices among companies; you can do so easily on the Internet and even make your reservations online. Drivers must be over 25 years old, carry a valid Canadian, US, or International Driver's License, and have a credit card. Optional damage waivers increase the cost, so check with your insurance carrier if you aren't certain whether your regular coverage also includes rentals. Avis, Budget, Hertz, and Thrifty all operate on the airport premises, with more companies in town. A compact with automatic transmission will cost anywhere from $30 to $40 a day plus hefty taxes, and, if you rent from an airport branch, airport fees as well.

CLIMATE

Vancouver enjoys a temperate climate and a reputation for rain. Summers can be quite lovely, and you might even see T-shirts and shorts in October, although you'll always want a jacket in the evenings. Expect precipitation in the winter, but no snow in the city proper.

Average daily temperatures are:

	J	F	M	A	M	J	J	A	S	O	N	D
°C	5	7	10	14	18	21	23	23	18	14	9	6
°F	41	44	50	58	64	69	74	73	65	57	48	43

CLOTHING

This is a casual city, where exercise clothes take up the most space in people's closets. Unless you hope to impress the fit young things shooting pool in Yaletown or lining up outside certain clubs, don't worry too much about your wardrobe. Pack walking shoes, a light raincoat, and dressy casual clothes (if you plan to haunt the better restaurants). For the beaches and hotel pools, you might also want a bathing suit. If you will be traveling in the late fall or winter, warm gloves, a hat, and a coat will keep you happy.

CRIME AND SAFETY

Due in part to strict gun control laws, Vancouver is quite safe, even at night, in nearly every neighborhood. The majority of crimes are property related, so be sensible and don't leave valuables in your car. The diciest area for tourists is East Hastings Street between Chinatown and Gastown. These blocks are of great concern to the tourism industry, which is pushing City Hall to do something — exactly what, however, isn't clear. If you are on foot and want to walk from Gastown to Chinatown, take Carrall to East Pender. You'll still be panhandled, but not to any great extent. For a big city, there aren't the huge numbers of street people that you see elsewhere; most appear on Robson Street where the numbers of passersby is the greatest. Police patrol on bikes and are easy to spot. In case of emergency, calling 911 will dispatch the police, an ambulance, or the fire department.

CUSTOMS AND ENTRY FORMALITIES

Visitors from the US require a birth certificate or some other evidence of citizenship (such as a passport) to cross the border. Visitors from Australia, France, Ireland, New Zealand, and the United Kingdom require a valid passport. A visa is not necessary. Tourists traveling from South Africa will need a valid passport and a visa. You'll receive a customs declaration on the airplane to complete and present on your way through the airport. Travelers are limited in the amounts of cigarettes and alcohol they can bring into the country. For more specific rules, contact the Canada Customs Office, at (604) 666-0545, or on the Internet at www.ccra-adrc.gc.ca/customs.

D

DRIVING

Downtown Vancouver is laid out in a grid pattern; it's thus fairly simple to learn your way around. Three bridges — Burrard, Granville, and Cambie — cross False Creek to the rest of Vancouver's neighborhoods to the south. To reach North and West Vancouver, head north on West Georgia Street through Stanley Park and over the Lions Gate (First Narrows) Bridge. The direction cars take on the center lane on West Georgia as it approaches the park changes depending on traffic patterns, so watch the signals. Head in the opposite direction on West Georgia over the viaduct to reach Vancouver's East Side and Commercial Drive.

Road conditions. Roads are well-maintained, though signage is sporadic.

Rules and regulations. Cars are driven on the right side of the road, signs indicate local speed limits in kilometers per hour, and seat belts, both back and front, are mandatory.

Fuel costs. Fuel is sold by the liter (about $0.83–$0.89/liter for regular), and gasoline stations are numerous.

If you need help. If you are a member of an automobile association, check for reciprocal membership with the BCAA at (604) 293-2222.

Parking. There's lots of competition for metered street parking everywhere you go, but fortunately there are also a fair number of parking garages in all the major shopping districts. Hotels maintain garages, for which you'll be charged from $5 to $17 per day. The cheaper the hotel, the cheaper the parking. Some offer free parking.

Fluid measures

Distance

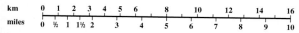

E

ELECTRIC CURRENT

Canada uses 110 or 120 volts, as in the US. The better hotels provide portable hair dryers, but if you are bringing electrical appliances from overseas, you'll need an adapter.

EMBASSIES and CONSULATES

Consul of Australia	1228-888 Dunsmuir Street Tel. (604) 684-1177
British Consulate General	800-1111 Melville Tel. (604) 683-4421
French Consulate General	1100-1130 West Pender Street Tel. (604) 681-4287
Consulate of Ireland	1400-100 West Pender Street Tel. (604) 683-9233
United States Consulate	1095 West Pender Street Tel. (604) 685-4311
New Zealand Consulate	1200-888 Dunsmuir Street Tel. (604) 684-7388

EMERGENCIES

Dial 911 in case of an emergency. If you are at your hotel, contact the switchboard.

G

GAY AND LESBIAN TRAVELERS

Vancouver is a highly tolerant community, and gay and lesbian visitors will feel perfectly comfortable. The West End of Vancouver (not to be confused with West Vancouver, which is across the Burrard

Inlet) has a large gay population. For information on events or entertainment geared toward the gay community, contact the Gay and Lesbian Centre at (604) 684-5307. A monthly community magazine, *Angles,* publishes articles and entertainment listings of interest.

GETTING THERE (see also AIRPORTS)

By Air. Vancouver International Airport, Canada's hub to Asia and the Pacific, is served by dozens of airlines, including Air New Zealand, British Airways, KLM, Lufthansa, and all the major US carriers. Over the Pacific, Air New Zealand flies from Auckland to Vancouver with one or two stops but no change of plane; Qantas offers a flight from Sydney with a change of plane in Honolulu; and United Airlines flies from Sydney to Vancouver with a stopover in San Francisco. Direct flights from Europe depart from London, Amsterdam, and Frankfurt. European travelers can also make connections through New York, Dallas, San Francisco, and other US hubs.

Helicopter service is available to Victoria through Helijet Airways (Tel. 1-800/665-4354 or 604/273-1414), as is seaplane service through Harbour Air seaplanes (604/688-1277). This is the fastest, but most costly, method of getting to Vancouver Island. Air Canada (Tel. 1-888-247-2262) also operates regular service.

By Rail. For information about train service through Canada, phone VIA Rail Canada, Inc., at 1-888-842-7245 or visit www.viarail.ca.

By Car. The US border is only one hour from Vancouver, and it takes about 2½ hours to drive from Vancouver to Seattle on Highway 99. Trans-Canada Highway 1 brings travelers into Vancouver from the east. Bring your passport.

By Sea. Vancouver is a popular cruise-line port and hosts dozens of ships between May and October. Ships dock downtown at the Canada Place Cruise Ship Terminal or at the Ballantyne Terminal, 10 minutes east of downtown.

GUIDED TOURS

Guided tours are great for an overview of urban centers, but they usually don't give visitors a chance to discover much other than tourist attractions. In any case, the city of Vancouver is best enjoyed on foot, outside the confines of buses or vans. However, if you don't plan to drive and you want to "do" Victoria, a bus tour is the most cost-effective way of getting there. Gray Line (604/879-3363 or toll-free: 800/667-0882) and Pacific Coach Lines (604/662-8074/ or 800/661-1725) are two of the major operators.

Walking Tours. Gassy Jack's statue at Water and Carrall streets in Gastown is the meeting place for a free 90-minute guided walking tour of Vancouver's oldest neighborhood (summer only). Tour starts at 2pm daily, rain or shine. Phone (604) 683-5650 for information.

Boat Tours. To see the city at its best, you'll need to spend some time on the water. On one end of the spectrum is a quick and inexpensive ride on the SeaBus to Lonsdale Quay. On the other is a do-it-yourself paddle around English Bay in a rental kayak (English Bay Sea Kayaking Company; Tel. 604/688-5770). In between are boat charter companies, many of which are located in Coal Harbour. One outfit, Harbour Cruises, Ltd. (Tel. 1-800-663-1500 or 604/688-7246), offers sunset dinner cruises, harbor tours and other jaunts.

H

HEALTH AND MEDICAL CARE

Hospitals. Hospitals are located all around Vancouver for urgent medical care. St. Paul's is downtown at 1081 Burrard Street (604/682-2344), with a 24-hour emergency room. Hospitals will not bill insurance carriers, so be prepared to pay with cash or a credit card for treatment; a visit will cost around $300.

Drugstores (Pharmacies). For over-the-counter drugs, there are two drugstore/pharmacies located on Robson Street and one in the

Pacific Centre Mall on West Georgia. Certain drugs require a doctor's prescription, so inquire with the pharmacist if you don't find what you are looking for on the shelves.

HITCHHIKING

It is illegal to pick up hitchhikers in British Columbia or to hitchhike on freeways. It is especially unwise for women to hitchhike, as prostitutes use this method to solicit business.

 L

LANGUAGE

English is the primary language spoken in Vancouver. Mandarin and Cantonese are the languages of choice in the suburb of Richmond.

LAUNDRY AND DRY CLEANING

Most hotels provide same-day laundry and dry cleaning services, but at a premium price. Your hotel desk clerk can direct you to a self-service laundromat.

LEGAL HOLIDAYS

Banks, businesses, and government offices are closed on these major Canadian holidays.

New Year's Day	1 January
Good Friday	Date varies in the spring
Easter Monday	Follows Good Friday
Victoria Day	Third Monday in May
Canada Day	1 July
British Columbia Day	First Monday in August
Labour Day	First Monday in September
Thanksgiving Day	Second Monday in October
Remembrance Day	11 November
Christmas Day	25 December
Boxing Day	26 December

M

MAPS

Your hotel concierge or desk clerk will give you a basic map of the city upon request. More detailed maps can be purchased at Vancouver Travel InfoCentre (1055 Dunsmuir Street, tel. 604 683-2000) and at the BC Automobile Association (999 West Broadway).

MEDIA

In print. For the best local entertainment listings, pick up a free copy of the *Georgia Straight* at your hotel, in many restaurants, and in bookstores; it is published every Thursday. The Vancouver edition of *Where* magazine also features listings. For informative articles on the region and its culture, check out *Vancouver Magazine* or its website: www.vanmag.com. Vancouver publishes two major daily newspapers: *The Vancouver Sun* and *The Province*. Canada's national newspaper is *The Globe and Mail*. Any of these can be purchased from sidewalk coin boxes, news vendors, or your hotel. International newspapers can be found at Mayfair News in the Royal Centre mall at Burrard and Georgia Streets.

Television. Check the local papers for program listings. Many channels available in Vancouver actually broadcast from Washington State in the US. If you seek local programming, click channels 3 (Vancouver CBC), 4 (Community TV), and 13 (CKVU Vancouver).

Radio. There are many AM and FM stations in Vancouver. For local news turn to AM 690 or AM 980.

MONEY MATTERS

Currency. Canadian currency is based on dollars and cents. One-dollar coins are called "loonies," after the bird pictured on the front, and two-dollar coins are called "twonies." There are 100 cents in a dollar.

Currency exchange. While US dollars are accepted at most business establishments, the exchange rate won't be as high as you'd get at a bank. Banks located in the financial center downtown charge a small fee to exchange American dollars, but banks outside the downtown corridor do not. For other foreign currency exchange, major downtown banks generally operate foreign currency departments. Bank hours vary, but most are open Monday through Friday from 9am to 5pm. Other currency exchange offices include American Express (1040 West Georgia Street), open Monday–Friday from 8:30am to 5:30pm and Saturday from 10am to 4pm; Thomas Cook Foreign Exchange (617 Granville Street), open Monday–Saturday from 9am to 5pm; and Bank of America at the Vancouver International Airport, open daily from 6:15am to 8pm.

Credit cards and ATMs. Major credit cards are accepted nearly everywhere and provide the best rate of exchange. You'll need a credit card to rent a car and make hotel reservations. ATMs are readily available and convenient for obtaining cash at all hours, but remember that you'll probably be charged a transaction service fee by your bank as well as by the local bank.

Traveler's checks. Traveler's checks are accepted in most establishments, but you might be asked for identification.

Taxes. Provincial sales tax (PST) of 7 percent is added to all purchases with the exception of books, magazines, and some groceries. In addition, a GST (goods and services tax) of 7 percent is added to everything but groceries. Hotels tack on an extra 10 percent for an accommodations tax as well.

You can get the GST portion refunded on goods over $50 and on accommodations, but not for car rentals, restaurants, or other services. Obtain a GST refund form from your hotel or any store. You will need to fill in the form and send it with your original receipts to Revenue Canada; you'll receive a refund check within four to six weeks. A few counters in the airport and shops around town advertise GST refunds on the spot, but they charge 15 percent of the proceeds.

OPEN HOURS

Shops. Store hours vary depending on the season, but stores are generally open Monday through Saturday from 10am to 6pm and Sunday from noon to 6pm. Stores located in shopping centers are often open until 9pm on Thursday, Friday, and Saturday nights, and many shops on Robson Street close closer to 10pm in the summer.

Government offices. Open Monday–Friday, 9am to 4:30pm.

Museums and tourist attractions. In July and August, most attractions are open seven days a week from 10am until 5pm or later. The rest of the year, some museums are closed one day during the week (usually Monday or Tuesday), and many are open late one evening per week for a reduced admission charge or even for free.

Restaurants. For the most part, Vancouverites don't eat fashionably late. Dinner is consumed anywhere from 6:30pm until 9:30pm, although you can find places that serve food up until midnight. The drinking age in British Columbia is 19.

Banks. Hours vary, but most are open Monday to Friday from 9am to 5pm, and some for limited hours on Saturday.

POLICE

For police, Highway Patrol, fire, or ambulance service in an emergency, telephone 911. You'll find that the police are polite and helpful.

POST OFFICES

The main post office is located at 349 West Georgia Street, and it is open Monday–Friday from 8am to 5:30pm. You can purchase stamps and send letters and parcels from any post office. Some newsstands also sell stamps.

PUBLIC TRANSPORTATION

Buses. The bus system in Vancouver is quite thorough. The Vancouver Regional Transit System includes buses, the SkyTrain, and the SeaBus to Lonsdale Quay. For routes and information, pick up a free copy of *Discover Vancouver* at any public library, information center, or terminal. Fares depend on the number of zones crossed. The basic fare is $1.75, but during rush hour (weekdays before 9:30am and weekday afternoons between 3 and 6:30pm) the fare for outlying zones increases to $2–$3. You will need exact change to purchase a ticket on the bus, or you can buy tickets and passes from retailers that display the blue-and-red "Faredealer" sign or from machines at SkyTrain and SeaBus depots. Transfers or validated tickets are good for 90 minutes in any direction, on any part of the system; for example, your SeaBus ticket is also valid on the bus or SkyTrain within the designated time period.

SkyTrain. This partially elevated rapid transit system operates every 3 to 5 minutes but only runs on one line. If you don't have a car, you might use SkyTrain to get to Science World or for a short tour of the city.

SeaBus. These passenger-only ferries cross Burrard Inlet every 15 minutes during the day and are a scenic and inexpensive way to see the harbor. Connecting buses await at the Lonsdale Quay terminal.

AquaBus. Tiny motorized ferries ply False Creek from the Hornby Street dock to Granville Island, Yaletown, Stamp's Landing, and Science World. Fares begin at $3 for adults and $1 for children.

BC Ferries. Operated by the Province of British Columbia, huge ferry boats accommodate buses, trucks, automobiles, bicycles, and passengers on foot. They offer snack bars, video games, and plenty of gorgeous scenery. Schedules are available from your hotel concierge or desk clerk, at the ferry terminals, and at tourist information centers (see page 122). Visitors going to Vancouver Island (Victoria) leave from Tsawwassen, a 1½ hour drive from downtown Vancouver, for the 1½-hour voyage that ends at Swartz Bay. Sunshine Coast ferries leave from Horseshoe Bay in West Vancouver and dock at Bowen Island, Langdale, and Departure Bay, near Nanaimo. Passenger fares are based on distance and are higher during the summer and on weekends. Major credit cards, traveler's checks, and cash are accepted.

Taxis. Because the fares include GST and start at $2, taxis are an expensive method of transportation. You can catch a taxi easily at any major hotel, or you can telephone one of several companies: Yellow Cab at (604) 681-1111, Vancouver Taxi at (604) 711-1111, or Black Top at (604) 731-1111.

R

RELIGIOUS SERVICES

Just about every religion is represented in Vancouver. For a listing of services, ask at your hotel or check the entry "Churches" in the yellow pages of the local telephone directory for the number of your preferred place of worship.

S

SMOKING

Smoking is prohibited inside restaurants and public buildings. It is currently allowed in bars and designated smoking areas, such as cigar lounges. Before lighting up in a taxi, ask the driver. The larger hotels have designated smoking floors. If the reservations agent forgets to ask if you prefer a smoking or non-smoking room, you should mention it if it makes a difference to you.

T

TELEPHONE

The area code for the metropolitan Vancouver area is 604; for Vancouver Island and the rest of British Columbia, it is 250. To place a local call within the metropolitan Vancouver area, simply dial the seven-digit number. To call outside the area, first dial 1, the area code, and then the seven-digit number. From outside North America, dial the international access code (011) first, then follow the instructions above. The major hotels and airlines have toll-free "1-800" numbers for reservations, but some work only within the US or Canada.

Pay phones can be spotted on the street, inside restaurants, and in hotels. Local calls cost $0.25. If you use a calling card, be advised that your long-distance carrier likely charges a premium for the privilege. Check beforehand to avoid surprises on your bill. If you phone from your hotel room, you will also be charged an extra fee, probably $1 per call.

TICKETS FOR EVENTS

For information on all the arts in Vancouver, call the Arts Hotline at (604) 684-2787, Monday–Saturday from 9am to 5:30pm. You can purchase tickets for events over the telephone with American Express, Visa, or MasterCard through Ticketmaster (Tel. 604/280-4444) or in person at the Ticketmaster outlet at 938 Howe Street in the Orpheum Theatre. Of course, tickets can also be purchased directly at theater box offices.

TIME ZONES

Vancouver is in the Pacific Time Zone, like the western United States. From April through October, Daylight Savings Time (DST) is adopted and clocks are set forward one hour.

Vancouver

Vancouver noon	New York 3pm	London 8pm	Paris 9pm	Sydney 7am

TIPPING

In general, tipping is expected in restaurants, bars, and taxis as well as for baggage handlers and tour guides. The rule of thumb is 15 percent or up to 20 percent for exceptional service.

Waiters/Waitresses	15 to 20 percent of the bill (before taxes)
Bartenders	$1 per round of drinks, more for a large crowd
Hotel/airline porters	$1 per bag
Hotel maid	$1 per day
Parking attendants	$1
Taxi drivers	15 percent
Tour guides	10 to 15 percent
Hairdressers/barbers	15 percent

TOILETS

Public toilets are readily available at gasoline (petrol) stations, at tourist attractions and parks, and in hotels and restaurants, although in the last instance you may need to be a customer to use one. You won't find attendants in any of these places as a rule, but you should find that facilities are well-maintained.

TOURIST INFORMATION OFFICES

Tourism Vancouver is a helpful source of information on Vancouver and the surrounding areas. Before your trip, request a copy of their *Vancouver Book* — a magazine actually — which contains an events calendar, hotel and restaurant listings, and information about the city. Their address is 200 Burrard Street, Suite 210, Vancouver, BC V6C 3LC, Canada; Tel. 1-800-663-6000 (in North America) or (604) 682-

2222 locally. In the UK, write to Tourism British Columbia, 1 Regent Street, London, England SW1Y 4NS, UK.

For information about Victoria, write to Tourism Victoria, 710-1175 Douglas Street, Victoria, BC V8W 2E1, Canada. For information about Whistler, write to Whistler Resort Association, 4010 Whistler Way, Whistler, BC V0N 1B4, Canada.

For additional Vancouver info, call or visit Tourism Vancouver's TouristInfo Centre at the Waterfront Centre (Plaza level) on Burrard St. (Tel.: 604/683-2000). In Victoria, the tourist information office is located across from the Empress Hotel on Government Street.

The web is also useful for reading up on the city, making rental car and airline reservations, and, in some cases, booking hotel rooms. The following websites are particularly well researched and up-to-date, providing links to other useful pages including Vancouver weather and BC Transit:

www.discovervancouver.com: Great design and content from the publisher of *The Greater Vancouver Book*, an urban encyclopedia.

www.tourismvancouver.com: The official city tourist site.

www.vancouver.bc.com: Useful but very commercial.

www.vanmag.com: This is the site of *Vancouver Magazine*, with penetrating food and entertainment guides and regional articles.

www.city.victoria.bc.ca: Victoria's official city site, with good links.

www.hellobc.com: British Columbia's official site and guide.

www.mybc.com: The site produced by BC Telephone is thorough, with Canadian stock quotes, and numerous listings, including phone.

W

WEIGHTS AND MEASURES

Canada uses the international metric system. For US travelers to Canada, some approximate equivalents are as follows: 1 US gallon is about 4 liters; 1 mile equals 1.6 kilometers; and 1 pound equals

Vancouver

0.45 kilograms. An easy way to translate temperature from Celsius to Fahrenheit is to multiply the degrees Celsius by 2 and add 30 (for example, 8°C=46°F).

Length

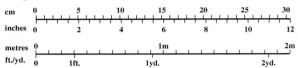

Weight

Temperature

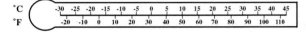

YOUTH HOSTELS

If you are interested in staying at any of the many youth hostels around British Columbia, it's best to purchase an International Youth Hostel card before your arrival. All BC hostels belong to the International Youth Hostel Federation. In Vancouver, budget travelers can enjoy million-dollar views for $21.50 per night (non-members) during peak season at the Jericho Beach Hostelling International/Vancouver (1515 Discovery; Tel. 1-888-203-4303). Hostelling International's downtown property (1114 Burnaby Street, Tel. 1-888-203-4302) has recently been renovated and costs $24 per night (non-members). See their website at www.hihostels.bc.ca for other locations, including Victoria and Whistler.

Recommended Hotels

Vancouver developers are busily adding a few thousand rooms to accommodate the influx of travelers arriving year 'round. Once the dust settles, visitors may see a drop in the high-season room rates. Prices are steep between May and October. The slower fall and winter months find Vancouver promoting attractive hotel packages that feature discounted rooms plus theater tickets or dining deals.

In general, BC hoteliers maintain excellent standards of cleanliness and service. Rooms usually include cable TV, direct-dial phones, and air conditioning, and if there is no concierge, the desk clerks will strive to provide directions and information. You must book in advance during the high season—the earlier the better. There are often discounts for Internet booking. For late reservations, call 1-800-HELLOVC (locally: 604/663-6000), or visit www.hellovc.com.

The stars below refer to high-season rack rates for a standard double room, exclusive of taxes (15–17 percent). Prices are in Canadian dollars without breakfast or parking unless noted. When making reservations at the larger hotels, always inquire about weekend packages, special promotions, and discounts even during the summer. Toll-free numbers are effective only within North America unless indicated otherwise. A plus (+) means "and up."

$$$$$	above $250
$$$$	$200–$250
$$$	$150–$200
$$	$125–$150
$	below $125

STANLEY PARK

Coast Plaza Suite Hotel $$$$$ *1763 Comox Street, Vancouver, BC V6G 1P6; Tel. (604) 688-7711, toll-free 1-800-663-1144; fax (604) 688-5934.* Views at this newly renovated

West End high-rise are lovely, especially from rooms facing nearby Stanley Park. Just off lively Denman Street. Spacious accommodations (the majority of which are suites), most with kitchens. Indoor pool, saunas, exercise room, two restaurants, and low-key atmosphere. 267 rooms. Major credit cards.

Sylvia Hotel $$$ *1154 Gilford Street, Vancouver, BC V6G 2P6; Tel. (604) 681-9321; fax (604) 682-3551.* The dowdy Sylvia, housed in an historic eight-story stone building just two blocks from Stanley Park, is one of the more sought-after addresses in the city. Yes, the rooms are plain, the bathrooms small and old-fashioned, and the lobby could stand a redo, but the location is superb and the price is right. Summer visitors should book a year in advance. 120 rooms. Major credit cards.

Westin Bayshore $$$$$ *1601 Bayshore Dr., Vancouver, BC V6G 2V4; Tel. (604) 682-3377, toll-free 1-800-WESTIN1; fax (604) 687-3102.* Corporate resort hotel overlooking Coal Harbour, with exquisite views. With 26 meeting rooms; full health club, (with massage therapist), indoor and outdoor pools, and two restaurants. The location between Stanley Park and downtown is unbeatable. Wheelchair accessible. 510 rooms. Major credit cards.

DOWNTOWN

Barclay Hotel $+ *1348 Robson Street, Vancouver, BC V6E 1C5; Tel. (604) 688-8850; fax (604) 688-2534.* A budget hotel in a Heritage building featuring small rooms furnished with the basics. Location on busy Robson Street will appeal to walkers and people watchers; balmy summer nights bring out the crowds, so expect a little noise. Restaurant and bar on premises. 85 rooms. Major credit cards.

Burrard Motor Inn $ *1100 Burrard Street, Vancouver, BC V6Z 1Y7; Tel. (604) 681-2331, toll-free 1-800-663-0366; fax*

(604) 681-9753. Pleasant three-story motor inn in a good location, just two blocks from Robson Street. Rooms are simple and comfortable, some with kitchenettes, appropriate for visitors on a budget. Pleasant outdoor patio. Restaurant and lounge in hotel. Complimentary parking. 71 rooms. Major credit cards.

Four Seasons $$$$$ *791 West Georgia Street, Vancouver, BC V6C 2T4; Tel. (604) 689-9333, toll-free 1-800-332-3442; fax (604) 684-4555*. Looming above the Pacific Centre mall, this AAA five-diamond luxury hotel has a reputation for fine service. Health club, indoor/outdoor pool, 24-hour room service. The main restaurant (of three), Chartwells, is highly praised. 385 rooms including 91 suites. Major credit cards.

Georgian Court Hotel $$$+ *773 Beatty Street, Vancouver, BC V6B 2M4; Tel. (604) 682-5555, toll-free 1-800-663-1155; fax (604) 682-8830*. Intimate, upscale hotel offers much value for the money. Rooms exude warmth and comfort. Fitness center, four restaurants. Centrally located, close to Yaletown, BC Place and the Queen Elizabeth Theatre. Wheelchair accessible. 180 rooms. Major credit cards.

Hotel Georgia $$$$ *801 W. Georgia Street, Vancouver, BC V6C 1P7; Tel. (604) 682-5566, toll-free 1-800-633-1111* The Crowne Plaza chain took over management of this 1927 property in 1998. Expensive renovation, with impressive lobby; bland rooms and baths are cell-like. Centrally located near downtown department stores. Fitness center and popular dance club (Elements) on site. 312 rooms. Major credit cards.

Comfort Inn Downtown $$-$$$ *654 Nelson Street, Vancouver, BC V6B 6K4; Tel. (604) 605-4333, toll-free 1-888-605-5333; fax (604) 605-4334*. Formerly Hotel Dakota. A 1904 building smartly renovated in 2001 into a trendy boutique hotel close to Yaletown and Granville Street cinemas. Small rooms simply but sleekly furnished with '50s-style blond wood and black-and-white photos. Gay friendly. Two popular night spots, Fred's Uptown Tavern and nightclub BaBalu, are connected. No views; reasonable parking fees. 100 rooms. Major credit cards.

Fairmont Hotel Vancouver $$$$+ *900 W. Georgia Street, Vancouver, BC V6C 2W6; Tel. (604) 684-3131, toll-free 1-800-441-1414; fax (604) 662-1929.* Elegant, landmark chateau-style building with a recent remodel. Those who can tear themselves away from one of the well-appointed guest rooms can make a vacation of wandering the lobby and shopping arcade, splashing about the spa and pool, or enjoying the hotel's two excellent restaurants. Wheelchair accessible. 556 rooms. Major credit cards.

Howard Johnson Hotel $-$$$ *1176 Granville Street, Vancouver, BC V6Z 1L6; Tel. (604) 688-8701, toll-free 1-888-654-6336; fax (604) 688-8335.* Formerly the Hotel Linden. The Howard Johnson chain recently assumed ownership of this newly renovated Heritage-style boutique hotel. Small-to-average guest rooms. Continental breakfast and complimentary use of fitness facilities across the street. Adjacent parking is only $8 per day. 110 rooms. Major credit cards.

Hyatt Regency Vancouver $$$$ *655 Burrard Street, Vancouver, BC V6C 2R7; Tel. (604) 683-1234, toll-free 1-800-233-1234; fax (604) 689-3707.* Excellent service, lovely décor, recent renovation but generic Hyatt charm. Popular destination for tour groups and business travelers, it's a good value considering the location. Standard guest rooms are large; for views, request an upper floor facing north. Fitness center and outdoor pool. Wheelchair accessible. 644 rooms; 35 suites. Major credit cards.

Listel $$$ *1300 Robson Street, Vancouver, BC V6E 1C5; Tel. (604) 663-5491, toll-free 1-800-663-5491; fax (604) 684-7092.* Subtle, stylish atmosphere contrasts sharply with the activity outside on a busy stretch of Robson. Original artwork in guest rooms on two "gallery" floors. Twice-daily maid service. Good restaurant with live jazz, indoor pool, gym, whirlpool, valet parking, many internet special rates. Wheelchair accessible. 130 rooms. Major credit cards.

Metropolitan Hotel $$$$-$$$$$ *645 Howe Street, Vancouver, BC V6C 2Y9; Tel. (604) 687-1122, toll-free 1-800-667-2300; fax (604) 643-7267.* Across from the Pacific Centre underground mall. Tasteful and quiet; luxurious décor has modern Asian touches. Gracious rooms, with cable TV. Swimming pool with a view; fitness center, sauna, whirlpool, excellent restaurant (Diva at the Met). 197 rooms. Major credit cards.

Pan Pacific $$$$$ *300–900 Canada Place, Vancouver, BC V6C 3B5; Tel. (604) 662-8111, toll-free 1-800-937-1515; fax (604) 685-8690.* Triple-A five-diamond hotel at Vancouver's convention center, made famous by photos of the five white sails floating elegantly over the harbor. Small guest rooms make the most of the unparalleled setting, all with luxurious amenities plus impeccable service. Health club, pool, services galore, car rental, and great views. 506 rooms. Major credit cards.

Riviera Hotel $-$$$ *1431 Robson Street, Vancouver, BC V6G 1C1; Tel. (604) 685-1301, toll-free 1-888-699-5222; fax (604) 685-1335.* A converted apartment building on the west end of Robson. Good views. Most units have kitchenettes; free parking. 40 rooms. Major credit cards.

Rosedale on Robson $$$$ *838 Hamilton Street, Vancouver, BC V6B 6A2; Tel. (604) 689-8033, toll-free 1-800-661-8870; fax (604) 689-4426.* All-suites hotel on a less frantic part of Robson Street offers the comforts of home. Helpful staff, a small playground, laundry facilities, exercise room, indoor pool, and a terrific location balance the ho-hum décor. A favorite with tour groups and airline personnel. Wheelchair accessible. 225 rooms. Major credit cards.

Vancouver

Sheraton Wall Centre **$$$$$** 1088 Burrard Street, Vancouver, BC V6Z 2R9; Tel. (604) 331-1000, toll-free 1-800-663-9255; fax (604) 331-1001. Corporate travelers and tour groups make good use of this big (and getting bigger), well-appointed glass-wall hotel with large cheerful rooms; the two-bedroom family suites make life on the road with kids almost pleasant. Quiet location a few blocks from boisterous Robson. Excellent concierge services. Wheelchair accessible. 455 rooms. Major credit cards.

Sutton Place **$$$$** *845 Burrard Street, Vancouver, BC V6Z 2K6; Tel. (604) 682-5511, toll-free 1-800-810-6888; fax (604) 682-5513.* A gracious and intimate AAA five-diamond hotel, with bright and spacious rooms and such amenities as thick terry robes, loofahs, and umbrellas. Twice-daily maid service, an excellent restaurant, European health spa, pool, and knowledgeable, friendly staff. Wheelchair accessible. 397 rooms. Major credit cards.

Fairmont Waterfront Centre **$$$$$** *900 Canada Place Way, Vancouver, BC V6C 3L5; Tel. (604) 691-1991, toll-free 1-800-441-1414; fax (604) 691-1828.* Beautifully designed hotel at the harbor has glorious views. Rooms are large, charmingly decorated in French-country prints, and contain all the amenities one expects from a fancy business hotel, including a fitness center and spa services. There is even an herb garden for guests to admire. Wheelchair accessible. 489 rooms. Major credit cards.

Wedgewood Hotel **$$$$+** *845 Hornby Street, Vancouver, BC V6Z 1V1; Tel. (604) 689-7777, toll-free 1-800-663-0666; fax (604) 608-5348.* Boutique hotel lavishly furnished with flowers, antiques and original art works. Prime location across from Robson Square and the Vancouver Art Museum. Twice-daily maid service, 24-hour room service, and an acclaimed restaurant (Bacchus). Wheelchair accessible. 51 rooms plus 34 suites. Major credit cards.

GRANVILLE ISLAND

Granville Island Hotel $$$ *1253 Johnston Street, Vancouver, BC V6H 3R9; Tel. (604) 683-7373, toll-free 1-800-663-1840; fax (604) 683-3061.* The unusual location on lively Granville Island provides nearly everything one needs—shopping, eateries, walking-distance attractions, and AquaBus transportation. Nicely decorated rooms with hair dryers, irons and Internet access, have marble floors and views. Adding 30 more rooms in August 2001. Wheelchair accessible. 54 rooms. Major credit cards.

NORTH VANCOUVER

Lonsdale Quay $$+ *123 Carrie Cates Court, North Vancouver, BC V6M 3K7; Tel. (604) 986-6111, toll-free 1-800-836-6111; fax (604) 986-8782.* For a different perspective on the city, travel across Burrard Inlet to this likable little hotel above the Lonsdale Quay Public Market where the view is Vancouver (as long as you get a south-facing unit). Standard room amenities, and transportation options are great: the SeaBus whisks you to town in 15 enjoyable minutes. 70 rooms. Major credit cards.

WEST VANCOUVER

Park Royal Hotel $$$ *540 Clyde Avenue, West Vancouver, BC, V7T 2J7; Tel. (604) 926-5511, toll-free 1-877-926-5511; fax (604) 926-6082.* If you're interested in hiking or skiing Grouse or Cypress Mountains, or if you'd rather stay outside the city closer to Horseshoe Bay, this charming small hotel is warm and inviting. Although it's located next to a busy highway, the park-like grounds offer serenity, and rooms are cozy, quiet, and attractively furnished. 30 rooms. Major credit cards.

WHISTLER

The Whistler Resort Association will assist in making reservations in any of the 115 hotels, condos, and B&Bs in the area. The toll-free number is 1-800-944-7853; locally, call (604) 664-5625.

Chateau Whistler (Fairmont) $$$$$ *4599 Chateau Boulevard, Whistler, BC V0N 1B4; Tel. (604) 938-8000, toll-free 1-800-441-1414; fax (604) 938-2020.* Part of the Canadian Pacific Hotels group (which includes the Fairmont Hotel Vancouver, Waterfront Centre, and the Empress), this 11-year-old ski and golf resort has won many travel industry awards. Elite, expensive, and full of amenities. Skiers should check out the low-season ski packages. Wheelchair accessible. 563 rooms. Major credit cards.

Holiday Inn SunSpree Resort $$$+ *4295 Blackcomb Way, Whistler, BC V0N 1B4; Tel. (604) 938-0878, toll-free 1-800-229-3188; (worldwide) 1-800-HOLIDAY; fax (604) 938-9943.* A cross between a hotel and a condominium complex, this inn will appeal to skiers and families taking a long vacation in Whistler. Studios and one- and two-bedroom suites include kitchens, although room service, of course, is only a phone call away. Fitness center and whirlpool. 114 rooms. Major credit cards.

VANCOUVER ISLAND

Abigail's Hotel $$$-$$$$+ *906 McClure Street, Victoria, BC V8V 3E7; Tel. (250) 388-5363, toll-free 1-800-561-6565; fax (250) 388-7787.* This Tudor-style inn three blocks from the harbor is a sanctuary for couples. The beautifully appointed rooms include private baths; some also have fireplaces and Jacuzzi tubs. The service is comparable to that of a much larger hotel, but here guests have the pleasure of a hearty breakfast included in the rates. 16 rooms. Major credit cards.

The Empress (Fairmont) $$$$$ *721 Government Street, Victoria BC V8W 1W5; Tel. (250) 384-8111, toll-free 1-800-441-1414; fax (250) 389-2747.* Once the beloved dowager of Victoria, where gloved and hatted ladies took tea amid brocade and antiques, the 91-year-old landmark remains the focal point of the city. A $50 million renovation in 1988 enlarged but some-what depersonalized this icon. Yet it still evokes a longing for civility, as evidenced by the 150,000 afternoon teas poured each year. Wheelchair accessible. 460 rooms. Major credit cards.

Holland House Inn $$$ *595 Michigan Street, Victoria, BC V8V 1S7; Tel. (250) 384-6644, toll-free 1-800-335-3466; fax (250) 384-6117.* Two houses (one brand new) connected by an inner patio form this serene, three-story decorator showcase that's a short walk from the harbor. Perfect for couples (children are discouraged), the large inviting rooms sport canopy beds, fireplaces, and antiques; some have jacuzzis. Gourmet breakfast included. Wheelchair accessible. 17 rooms. Major credit cards.

James Bay Inn $ *270 Government Street, Victoria, BC V8V 2L2; Tel. (250) 384-7151, toll-free 1-800-836-2649; fax (250) 385-2311.* The artist Emily Carr spent her last years at this pleas-ant inn with bay windows while it was an old-age home. Renovated in 1998, it's the third oldest operating hotel in the city and just four blocks from downtown. Budget-minded trav-elers will be pleased with the simple but tasteful rooms. Discounts for longer stays. 43 rooms. Major credit cards.

Sooke Harbour House $$$$$ *1528 Whiffen Spit Road, Sooke, BC V0S 1N0; Tel. (250) 642-3421; toll free, 1-800-889-9688; fax (250) 642-6988.* This romantic, secluded slice of par-adise will remind you that life indeed can be extraordinary, from the fresh flowers to the original artwork lavished around every room. Rates include breakfast, to be enjoyed in front of your fireplace, on your balcony overlooking the ocean, or perhaps in bed. Wheelchair accessible. 28 rooms. Major credit cards.

Recommended Restaurants

When a neighborhood restaurant has a dozen customers waiting patiently on the sidewalk for a table on a rainy Monday night in November, you can be certain you've arrived in a town that enjoys its food. Don't waste a meal while in Vancouver. The local ingredients are too tasty, the chefs are too passionate, and the energy is too enticing for you to end up in some tired concept restaurant with a menu specializing in boredom.

Along with the picks described below, find reliable dining recommendations in *City Foods* or in James Barber's *"I Love Good Food" Guide to Eating in Vancouver.* Your hotel's concierge staff is another source, but be advised that they probably work from a patronage list. Do be sure to make dinner reservations, which are essential in many places. Unless otherwise indicated, restaurants are open for lunch as well as dinner.

The price categories below indicate the approximate cost of a three-course meal, per person, excluding drinks. Taxes (7 percent) and tips (15 percent) will add to your bill. Note that wine is especially expensive in Vancouver due to high excise taxes.

$$$	Over $40
$$	$20–$40
$	under $20

DOWNTOWN

Allegro Café $$ *888 Nelson Street; Tel. (604) 683-8485.* Moderately priced Italian food in a spot the local cognoscenti have adopted. Notable soups, pastas, and deftly prepared entrées.

Don't let the upstairs location in an office building turn you off. Closed Sundays; closed for lunch on Saturdays. Major credit cards.

Bandi's $$ *1427 Howe Street; Tel. (604) 685-3391.* If you're looking for European home cooking, you won't find a more authentic place to sup on Hungarian sour cherry soup and goulash. Located in a charming old home set back from the street, it's a bit like eating at grandmother's house. Closed for lunch Saturdays and Sundays. Major credit cards.

C Restaurant $$$ *1600 Howe Street; (604) 681-1164.* Some folks are reluctant to order sea bass accompanied with gooseneck barnacles, but customers who stick around long enough to see if the kitchen is serious are in for a striking experience. This sophisticated, innovative patio seafood restaurant on False Creek delivers food that is as beautiful and flavorful as it is unusual. The menu always includes something understandable for seafood lovers. Major credit cards.

Hermitage $$$ *109-1025 Robson Street; Tel. (604) 689-3237.* Warm brick décor and French-influenced cooking combine to keep voices lowered and manners intact. Set in a courtyard off busy Robson, the patio is a quiet respite. Major credit cards.

Diva at the Met $$$ *645 Howe Street; Tel. (604) 602-7788.* Elegant terraced room in the Metropolitan Hotel, with an eclectic menu featuring seafood, new North American cooking, and great desserts. First-rate service, a stellar reputation, and the use of what's seasonal keep Diva at the top of the "Best of" lists. Stylish bar with food service toward the front in case you forgot to make reservations. Open for breakfast. Major credit cards.

Earl's on Top $ *1185 Robson Street; Tel. (604) 669-0020.* If you arrive in Vancouver tired and hungry and you want a quick bite before calling it a night, any of the Earl's chain of restaurants are acceptable easy places to eat, especially with children. Quality, imaginative food for the price; terrace dining available in summer. Major credit cards.

Étoile $$$ *1355 Hornby Street; Tel. (604) 681-4444.* A tiny, romantic space serving exquisite modern French food. The three-course prix fixe menu, which changes nightly, is a remarkable bargain and should not be missed. Specialties: Alaskan sea scallops and roast duck. The wine list is small but thoughtfully well-chosen. Open for lunch Fridays only. Major credit cards.

Fleuri $$$ *Sutton Place Hotel, 845 Burrard Street; Tel. (604) 642-2900.* An exceptional hotel dining room. The surroundings are comfortable yet plush; a pianist plays standards in the background, and the Pacific Northwest menu is enticing and well-executed, featuring roasted rack of lamb with a lavender and grapefruit crust Chocolate dessert buffet served Thursday through Saturday nights. Major credit cards.

Hy's Encore $$$ *637 Hornby Street; Tel. (604) 683-7671.* This is the place to go for an old-fashioned char-broiled steak dinner with a Caesar salad constructed table-side, big baked potato, and all the trimmings. A Vancouver tradition. Closed for lunch Saturdays and Sundays. Major credit cards.

Il Giardino di Umberto $$$ *1382 Hornby Street; Tel. (604) 669-2422.* A table on the patio on a warm summer day, something savory from the outdoor brick oven, a glass of red wine, and your vacation has reached its peak. Inside, glance at the power lunchers dealing over fancy bowls of pasta. At night, savor romance in one of the prettiest dining rooms outside Tuscany. Closed Sundays, lunch Saturdays. Major credit cards.

Shanghai Chinese Bistro $ *1128 Alberni Street; Tel. (604) 683-8222.* Tasty Cantonese and Szechuan dishes, featuring an extensive selection of fresh seafood and shellfish. Chefs make noodles from scratch in front of diners; if you haven't ordered any, you'll wish you had. Great for dim sum at lunch. Located on the second floor of a nondescript building. Open until 1am weekends. Major credit cards.

Yaletown Brewing Co. $ *1111 Mainland Ave; Tel. (604) 681-2739.* Brick walls and denim-covered banquettes define the casual atmosphere of this noisy (9 TVs), popular brew-pub on a Yaletown corner. Burgers, pasta, pizza, and daily specials prepared in an open kitchen in the main room; large selection of house-brewed beers such as Frank's Nut Brown Ale and wheat beers on tap. Major credit cards.

EAST OF DOWNTOWN

Havana $ *1212 Commercial Drive; Tel. (604) 253-9119.* The food, which starts with breakfast and ends with dinner, has an Afro-Latino flavor, but may not be the main reason to make your way to the Grandview neighborhood on the East Side. Consider your time here a funky cultural diversion. Order an excellent coffee, eat if you're hungry, and drink in Vancouver as seen from one of its coolest districts. Major credit cards.

Pink Pearl $ *1132 East Hastings Street; Tel. (604) 253-4316.* The din from business-lunchers, Chinese families, and the dim sum trolley-carts rolling past the linen-covered tables creates the atmosphere in this cavernous, popular, award-winning Cantonese restaurant. Order off a lengthy menu, from the live seafood tank, or choose from a good variety of dim sum. Major credit cards.

WEST END AND STANLEY PARK

Café de Paris $$ *751 Denman Street; Tel. (604) 687-1418.* The leek and duck confit tart will have you speaking endearments to the chef. You'll fight your friends over the greaseless, crispy pommes frites on the table. This very French bistro is a delight and a bargain at lunch; you shouldn't miss it. Closed for lunch on Saturdays. Reservations essential. Major credit cards.

Vancouver

Cardero's $$ *1583 Coal Harbour Quay; Tel. (604) 669-7666.*
A spacious and casual restaurant with a menu that seeks to please a spectrum of tastes. Burgers, pizza, and pasta should keep the kids calm. Salads, the usual fish choices, and gourmet steak dishes cover the needs of those with bigger appetites. Windows frame breathless North Vancouver and harbor views. Great bar. Major credit cards.

Fish House in Stanley Park $$ *8901 Stanley Park Drive; Tel. (604) 681-7275.* The location, by the English Bay entrance to the park, is a draw in itself. Specialty: tiger prawns sautéed with garlic, roasted red peppers, tomatoes and feta cheese, flambéed with ouzo; also classics such as an ahi tuna steak "Diane," and a seductive fresh oyster bar. Major credit cards.

Raincity Grill $$ *1193 Denman Street; Tel. (604) 685-7337.*
An urban bistro space across from English Bay with entrancing views, especially at sunset. The sophisticated Pacific Northwest cuisine features whatever's fresh, and the wine list is renowned. Portions are generous, so don't bring delicate eaters or children here. Major credit cards.

Teahouse in Stanley Park $$$ *7510 Stanley Park Drive (Ferguson Point); Tel. (604) 669-3281.* The garden-party surroundings, with mesmerizing views of English Bay, are so warm and inviting that you want to make your meal last as long as possible. But that takes great self-control when faced with the seared beef salad or potato-crusted sea bass, or the eggs Benedict with bacon at brunch. Major credit cards.

GRANVILLE ISLAND

Bridges $$ *1696 Duranleau Street; Tel. (604) 687-4400.* More terrific views, day and night. A $50 prix fixe dinner menu offers a wide variety of local delicacies with a seafood accent, and dessert. Also features dockside bistro wine bar for casual (under $20) dining, outdoor dining and pub as well as a Sunday Brunch. Major credit cards.

Dockside Brewing Company $$ *Granville Island Hotel, 1253 Johnston Street; Tel. (604) 685-7070.* A jaded young Vancouver businesswoman described this place as "amazing," and she wasn't talking about the unique views of False Creek. The excellent menu touches on all the basics but leans toward seafood. The handcrafted lagers and ales taste even better when sipped on the patio with some grilled red curry prawns. Major credit cards.

WEST SIDE

Bishop's $$$ *2183 West 4th Avenue; Tel. (604) 738-2025.* Bishop's remains at the pinnacle of the fine dining experience in Vancouver, with seasonal ingredients prepared simply and with the utmost regard for flavor. A special-occasion destination for the locals, and a must stop for gourmets. Major credit cards.

Lumière $$$ *2551 West Broadway; Tel. (604) 739-8185.* Immerse yourself in the freshest, loveliest local ingredients combined by a much-celebrated local chef to excite the palate and please the eye. Order from the "tasting menu" and settle in for a long, pleasurable evening. The modern setting is simple and comfortable. Open for dinner only; closed Mondays. Major credit cards.

Provence Mediterranean Grill $$ *4473 West 10th Avenue; (604) 222-1980.* This Point Grey neighborhood bistro fills with locals who appreciate the moderate prices and the tasty French (with a dollop of Italian) menu. Colorful, fresh antipasti make for a light starter; the crisp roasted chicken couldn't be better on a cold night. Hold out for a patio table at lunch on a sunny Vancouver day. Major credit cards.

Sami's $ *986 West Broadway; Tel. (604) 736-8330.* Located in a tiny corner shopping center, friendly Sami's serves tasty Indian food with a fusion twist. Dishes to investigate include tender beef short ribs in cumin and ginger, and a fragrant basmati rice paella. A genuine bargain, the locals love it. Major credit cards.

Seasons in the Park $$ *Queen Elizabeth Park; Tel. (604) 874-8008.* Perched on the highest point in the city, all the tables here take advantage of the panoramic views of Vancouver and beyond. The straightforward menu features fresh fish, proper salads, and desserts such as lemon pie. Major credit cards.

Sophie's Cosmic Café $ *2095 West 4th Avenue; Tel. (604) 732-6180.* Eclectic and hip. You can order a big, delicious breakfast here that will keep you going almost until dinner, which Sophie's also serves. The wait on weekends can be long. The line starts at 9 am. A particularly smart choice for families. Major credit cards.

Tojo's $$$ *202-777 West Broadway, Suite 202; Tel. (604) 872-8050.* This dignified, innovative Japanese restaurant is reputed to have the best sushi to be found anywhere. Take a seat at the bar and let Tojo himself take your order. He's an innovative artist of sushi. If sushi is not your dish of saki, repair to the elegant tatami room, where you sit Japanese-style on cushions.

Vij's $$ *1480 West 11th Avenue; Tel. (604) 736-6664.* Diners patiently line up outside, knowing nothing is worth the wait like dinner at this innovative Indian bistro, where the menu changes monthly. Very highly recommended. Friendly service; etherial atmosphere. The house-made sparkling ginger lemon drink is a treat. Open for dinner only. No reservations. Major credit cards.

WEST VANCOUVER

The Beach House at Dundarave Pier $$$ *150 25th Street, West Vancouver; Tel. (604) 922-1414.* The heated oceanfront patio is but one of three dining levels from which to view magnificent Burrard Inlet in this elegant restaurant. Fresh main ingredients are presented with unusual flair, with accents such as basil red pepper crème and rosemary goat cheese. A tower of three cheesecakes dominates desserts. Major credit cards.

Beach Side Café $$ *1362 Marine Drive, West Vancouver; Tel. (604) 925-1945.* This is a wonderful location with a picture-postcard view of Vancouver's West Side. The bonus is a West Coast menu prepared with an experienced, deft hand. It's the kind of neighborhood restaurant that makes you fervently wish you lived around the block. Major credit cards.

BOWEN ISLAND

Beggar's Purse $$ *Orchard Square in Snug Cove; Tel. (604) 947-0550.* For a memorable evening, take the ferry from Horseshoe Bay to Bowen Island and walk up the main street to this cozy spot. A prix fixe menu highlights local ingredients. Reservations are a must. Open Thursday, Friday and Saturday nights, dinner only. Major credit cards.

VANCOUVER ISLAND

Café Brio $$ *944 Fort Street, Victoria; Tel. (250) 383-0009, toll-free 1-866-270-5461.* A few blocks from downtown in a handsome wrought-iron trimmed stucco house. Organically grown produce and fresh local ingredients combine to create a seasonally changing contemporary West Coast menu. Lively ambience. Closed for lunch on weekends. Major credit cards.

Sooke Harbour House $$$ *1528 Whiffen Spit Road, Sooke; Tel. (250) 642-3421.* The restaurant at this beautiful inn is a destination in itself. Named by The Globe and Mail as Canada's best restaurant in 1997, it's no stranger to travel magazine lists of the world's top spots. Meals here use vegetables, fruits, and berries grown at the inn, fish from the harbor, meat from Island producers, and other locally foraged items. Open for dinner only. Major credit cards.

INDEX